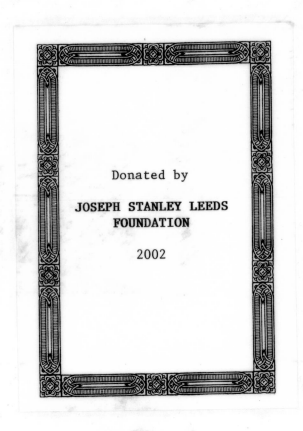

# ORIGAMI

# ORIGAMI

## THE COMPLETE GUIDE TO THE ART OF PAPERFOLDING

### RICK BEECH

LORENZ BOOKS

*To Sue, my inspiration,*
*with love and affection.*

First published by Lorenz Books in 2001

© Anness Publishing Limited 2001

Lorenz Books is an imprint of Anness Publishing Limited
Hermes House, 88–89 Blackfriars Road, London SE1 8HA

Published in the USA by Lorenz Books, Anness Publishing Inc.
27 West 20th Street, New York, NY 10011

www.lorenzbooks.com

This edition distributed in Canada by Raincoast Books
9050 Shaughnessy Street
Vancouver
British Columbia
V6P 6E5

A CIP catalogue record for this book is available from the British Library.

Publisher  Joanna Lorenz
Managing Editor  Judith Simons
Art Manager  Clare Reynolds
Project Editor  Charlotte Berman
Photography  John Freeman
Design  Penny Dawes
Jacket Design  Axis Design
Editorial Reader  Joy Wotton
Production Controller  Steve Lang

1 3 5 7 9 10 8 6 4 2

# contents

## The Projects

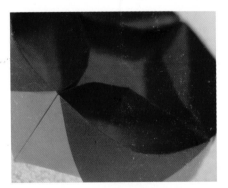

# introduction

Welcome to this comprehensive volume devoted to the beautiful ancient Japanese art of origami, or, as it may more commonly be known, paperfolding. In postwar England, enthusiasts were introduced to the art via the Rupert Bear annuals, which featured a character also illustrated in the *Daily Express*. The illustrations were by Alfred Bestall, who was a keen origami enthusiast, and he often introduced the art into the Rupert stories. Chance meetings with Japanese students or lovers of magic tricks and novelties also provided an introduction to origami. Many will remember seeing the inspiring television show hosted by Robert Harbin in the 1970s. However you discover the art, you will always be grateful that you did. Paperfolding is a delightful experience, an intellectual challenge, an entertainment, an opportunity to share ideas, and a thing of beauty, and therefore, according to Keats, "a joy for ever".

**ABOVE** Rupert Bear, folding an origami bird.

## What is origami?

Origami is the Japanese art of paperfolding, the name deriving from two Japanese words, "ori" meaning to fold, and "kami" meaning paper. Dictionaries often suggest that it is the art in which bird forms and other models are folded from paper. From this brief description or from childhood memories, you may be forgiven for thinking that origami is limited to paper planes, waterbombs and fortune tellers. As you will soon discover, the interest in traditional origami folding continues, but the art has also advanced considerably in the last 30 to 40 years, so that a paper representation of virtually anything is now possible.

Origami is not limited to using only paper. Over the years, enthusiasts throughout the world have experimented with all kinds of materials while still adhering to the principles of folding. Lane Allen (USA), for example, has introduced Orikane. This entails folding models from several varieties of fine metal gauze. This material has two obvious differences from standard origami paper: it can be moulded and curved, which opens up a variety of creative possibilities. Another American, Jeremy Shafer, designed a pair of working Nail Clippers; after folding the model from a very fine Japanese foil paper, he went on to develop a version made out of similarly fine metal sheeting. David Brill (UK) surprised the folding community several years ago with his Ship in a Bottle, which required the bottle to be made of something transparent; he found the ideal

**BELOW** Miniature origami models on display at The Origami Gallery in Tokyo.

RIGHT A life-size Tyrannosaurus Rex skeleton folded from 21 sheets of paper and created by Issei Yoshino in 1996. Pictured at the 2nd International Origami Festival in Charlotte, North Carolina, USA.

material in the non-sticky acetate sheet book covering sold in many stationers. This material is also used by Mette Pederson (USA), who folds several unit modular pieces of origami (solid geometric forms made by joining many individual pieces of paper), which she then encases in a clear outer shell. The Dutch are particularly fond of Teabag Folding where they create two-dimensional mosaic patterns from ornate tea-bag wrappers, while dinner-napkin folding has always been popular around the world. There are many materials that are suitable for folding, and you can have great enjoyment adapting what you will learn in this book to the sources you can find in the world around you.

It is also a common misconception that the paper always has to be a square. There are hundreds of designs using various rectangles, different regular polyhedra and even circles. Nor are you limited to the number of sheets of paper used for each design.

## What isn't origami?

Unlike other paper arts, origami is highly disciplined, in that only the paper folds create the subject. Indeed, purists will frown upon the mere mention of the words "cut" or "stick", and are unlikely to agree that the odd slit here and there to help make a fold possible is true origami. So, designing origami can be a complex procedure, as you try to realize your idea while taking account of the restrictions imposed by the medium.

## Materials

Paper is everywhere, and is among the cheapest and most common materials you can think of. It is available in a range of thicknesses and with a widely varying ability to hold creases, and so the choice of paper to use for origami is very important. Suggestions have been given for a suitable paper to use for each project, but your own experiments and initiative will be a factor as you practise folding more and more models. Do not be discouraged if you choose a particular kind of paper only to find that, for whatever reason, it is not really suitable for that project. In fact, you may need to fold two or three practice versions before deciding on the paper you feel is best for your final model.

You will become a paper connoisseur as you discover the wealth of choice while you shop around. Even if you have no immediate use for a particular paper, but love its colour or texture, buy it and add it to your collection. One day just the right model will come along.

# A History of the Art

With the advent of paper came paperfolding, and for over 2,000 years origami has been a source of interest, enjoyment and intellectual stimulation for adults and children alike. In recent times origami has also become an educational tool, and a symbol of peace and remembrance, while for millions of people all over the world paperfolding continues to be an unrivalled pastime.

# traditions and innovations

Paperfolding originated in China around the 1st or 2nd century AD, and reached Japan in the 6th century. It began as an art which, like many others in Japanese culture, was based on suggestion rather than realism: a few simple creases that evoked the spirit of an animal, a flower, or a bird, for example, rather than producing a detailed representation.

## The Japanese tradition

Over the following generations, origami would become familiar in many aspects of Japanese culture. By the Heian period, from 794–1185, origami was a significant part of the ceremonial life of the Japanese nobility. Samurai warriors would exchange gifts adorned with noshi – good luck tokens of folded paper and strips of abalone (shellfish) or dried meat. Shinto noblemen celebrated weddings with glasses of sake decorated with male and female paper butterflies, representing the bride and groom. Tea-ceremony masters received their diplomas specially folded for secrecy; once the wrapping had been opened, it could not be refolded without extra creases being added, which would show the document had already been seen.

When paper became inexpensive enough to be used by everyone, origami assumed a new ceremonial role, as a means of social stratification. During the Muromachi period, 1338–1573, origami styles served to distinguish classes among the aristocratic samurai. In the Tokugawa period, 1603–1867, a democratization of origami occurred, as Japanese art and culture

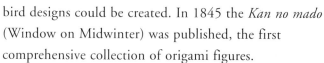

**RIGHT**
A contemporary version of a Japanese noshi.

**RIGHT** Ancient Japanese woodblock showing a magician who, according to legend, folded a flapping bird so realistic that it took flight.

blossomed. This period saw the emergence of the bird base as documented in the oldest surviving publication on origami, the *Senbazuru Orikata* (How to Fold a Thousand Cranes). A base is a set of folds, in this case representing a bird, from which other, more elaborate, bird designs could be created. In 1845 the *Kan no mado* (Window on Midwinter) was published, the first comprehensive collection of origami figures.

## A symbol of peace

After the atomic bomb was dropped on Hiroshima in 1945, killing over 75,000 people, radiation sickness and various forms of cancer began claiming even more lives. One such was Sadako Sasaki, who was diagnosed with leukaemia in 1955. She had been two years old at the time of the blast, and was apparently unhurt despite being only a mile and a half away from the epicentre of the explosion. Ten years later so many children were being diagnosed with leukaemia that it had become known as "A-bomb disease."

While Sadako was in hospital a friend folded her a traditional origami crane. This was a highly symbolic gift because the crane, which is a sacred bird in Japan, is believed to live for a thousand years and to have the power of granting wishes. Anyone who folds a thousand cranes will have their wish granted.

**ABOVE** The Children's Peace Monument at Hiroshima, which is annually draped with thousands of paper cranes.

Sadako began folding cranes with every bit of paper she could find. At first, all of her wishes were for health, but as she grew weaker, she began wishing instead for world peace. By the time she died, she had folded 644 cranes; her friends folded the remaining cranes. They later formed a club and began raising money for a monument. Students from over 3,000 schools in Japan and from nine other countries gave donations, and three years later, in 1958, the Children's Peace Monument was unveiled in Hiroshima's Peace Park. Now every year on 6 August, Peace Day is commemorated and people from all over the world send paper cranes to the park.

## A Moorish parallel

The Japanese were not the only ones to cultivate the art of paperfolding. It was developed simultaneously by the Moors, who took paperfolding to Spain during their invasion in the 8th century AD. The Moors were excellent

mathematicians and astronomers, and introduced the theory of paperfolding as an aid to teaching the principles of geometry. Their activity flourished in the 13th century and the traditions of paperfolding survive to the present day. It was practised and documented by the Spanish philosopher and poet Miguel de Unamuno (1864–1936).

## Origami today

In the West, origami gained the reputation of being little more than a child's pastime, and never achieved status as an art. For generations, European and American schoolchildren have grown up familiar with waterbombs and flapping birds, jumping frogs and fortune tellers. However, more recently, enthusiasts from all over the world have begun to recognize origami as an intellectual pursuit, as well as a highly creative and fashionable exercise.

In 1967 the British Origami Society in England was formed. It evolved from the Portfolio Society, which had a privately circulated newsletter. Following a suggestion by Tim Ward and Trevor Hatchett in the Southern Portfolio Notebook, it was decided that a new society should be formed for fellow origami enthusiasts, and a magazine produced to be distributed countrywide among its members.

The early days were very exciting for David Lister, Iris Walker, Sydney French and others, as they began to correspond with Lillian Oppenheimer in the United States of America, and Akira Yoshizawa in Japan, together with other devotees of the art. The boundaries in the complexity of origami creations began to broaden, and, by the mid-1970s, it was realized that different techniques and folding methods could be applied to the paper, whereas, in the past, only designs originating from traditional bases had been used.

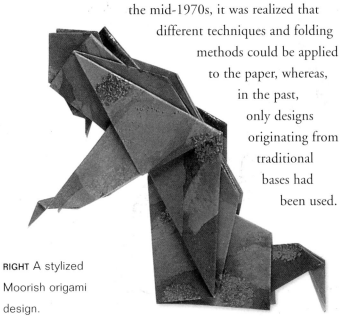

**RIGHT** A stylized Moorish origami design.

Several milestone discoveries, by folders such as Fred Rohm and Neal Elias in the United States, and Max Hulme and David Brill in the United Kingdom, proved that no subject was beyond tackling where an origami representation was concerned. Indeed, many modern enthusiasts began to create their own bases. This extended the variety of models that could be made.

Elias devised a system known as box-pleating, where the paper is collapsed into a concertina. By using 45-degree creases within these folds, a whole range of animals and human figures can be created. Sometimes more than one subject is produced from the same sheet of paper, for example, a Matador and Bull, Chinaman Pulling a Rickshaw, or a Mother with Pram. Rohm invented the Simplex base, which enabled an action model of a Snake Charmer with Snake to be folded. Competitions among creative designers have also progressed on to new heights: in the early 1990s a worldwide challenge was issued to designers to produce work on the theme of *Alice in Wonderland*. All models, whether individual pieces or collective dioramas, had to conform to Sir John Tenniel's drawings from the original Lewis Carroll books.

**ABOVE** Alfred Bestall, president of the British Origami Society (1978–1986), demonstrating the importance of perseverance and dedication.

**ABOVE** A fine example of modular folding; this example is by David Mitchell.

RIGHT The author (right) and Larry Hart producing a giant elephant to demonstrate the strength and durability of paper for a television show.

## From straight lines to soft curves

There is still, however, the "less-is-more" philosophy among many folders, due to the emphasis Western origami places on design technique rather than aesthetic beauty. So, while some prefer to fold the working Cuckoo Clock, designed by Robert Lang, out of one sheet of paper, others will derive greater satisfaction from making simple traditional folds and their many variations. Long-standing British Origami Society member, John Smith, has introduced what he terms Pureland Origami, where models are created using only valley folds. Paul Jackson is fascinated by the interaction of light and dark on simple folded forms and adopts a minimalist approach in his work. While it is technically challenging to produce a working jack-in-a-box, it is a different discipline to invent a simply stylized three-fold elephant.

Modular origami became popular in the early 1990s. It is a challenge to design complex origami models comprised of many units interlocked simply by inserting the point of one unit into the pocket of another. The interest and complexity in modular origami continues to escalate, so that some models, such as those by Tom Hull, consist of several hundred units.

Origami is, by its very nature, based on geometry – every crease is a straight line. This is a bonus when folding inanimate or stylized models, where the main objective is accuracy. However, for animate objects curved surfaces are the norm and straight lines the exception and in order to create a lifelike model a different approach is required.

The move into fully three-dimensional folding was initiated by the Japanese Master, Akira Yoshizawa. His overriding aim was to capture the essence of his subject rather than simply reproducing all the detailed features. To do this he introduced two key concepts, folding softly and wet folding.

Most origami projects require the folder to make each crease as sharp as possible so that there is either a firm crease or no crease at all. Yoshizawa suggested that some creases should be made more softly than others, allowing a finished model to possess a whole spectrum of creases, from sharp through to very gentle. However, the technical problem of adding gentle creases is that they do not readily stay in place, and therefore the completed works are fragile and temporary. Yoshizawa overcame this by wet folding:

**RIGHT** This life-size model of a rhinoceros by Eric Joisel was folded for the largest ever exhibition of origami at the Louvre in Paris in 1998. Because it was wet-folded it has a more realistic appearance.

folding with dampened paper which retained its shape when dried. The secret behind this technique lies in the water-soluble adhesive, called sizing, which binds the paper fibres together and provides the stiffness. Damping the paper dissolves the sizing, separating the fibres and leaving the paper floppy and malleable. As the paper dries out the fibres set in their new position.

Only paper with soluble sizing is appropriate, and, in general, the thicker types of paper are best, such as artist's Ingres paper. As a technique, however, wet folding is still shunned by many folders because of the associated drawbacks: dampened paper is difficult to handle and easy to tear. The loosened fibres will separate easily, especially where several layers need to be folded simultaneously. The paper also expands unevenly in the direction of the fibres, so accurate folding is also a problem. In addition, due to the thickness of the paper, it is difficult to make models that require complex folds or numerous layers of paper.

## What's the appeal?

Styles of origami come and go, and designers may concentrate on different aspects of the art at various times, producing work of a similar nature, be it animal folds, or modular. If you feel that you have it within you to try to invent your own models, remember that there seem to be two schools of thought among origami designers: there are

**ABOVE** Vase of flowers by Akira Yoshizawa, 1983.

**ABOVE** An origami decorated Christmas tree entrances shoppers in New York.

those that wake up one morning and declare their intention of designing an origami elephant. Then there are the others who play around with the paper until inspired as to what form it may later take. Both approaches can be equally satisfying.

Children love origami, so you will find it an invaluable skill when amusing the young. For the commuter and long-distance traveller, it is a great way to pass a journey, and you will find that if you fold while on a bus, a train, or when flying, it is not long before you have a transfixed audience. There is also much fun to be had in preparing practical origami for parties and other functions, and your guests will be impressed with your skill and dexterity.

Included in this volume are practical origami, decorations, action toys and challenging multi-piece modular unit origami. I hope you enjoy my selection.

## HOW TO USE THIS BOOK

Start at the beginning, and give yourself time to become familiar with all you need to know in preparation for model making. This includes studying the following sections on Techniques and Base Folds. Only when you have learned these procedures thoroughly can you confidently start making the designs in this book to a standard that will please and satisfy you. Each chapter is organized so that it begins with simple projects that progress towards more challenging designs. While you are folding, consider what is commonly known as the Look Ahead rule: when you are following individual illustrations, it is always wise to look two to three steps ahead, to see how things should turn out. Sometimes, even turn to the final steps for any particular model you might be folding, so that you can see the completed project; this will encourage you enormously. Do not allow yourself to become discouraged; persevere, try and try again, take your time, and enjoy your folding.

**RIGHT** A string of 1,000 cranes folded by members of the British Origami Society.

# A Gallery of Origami Masterpieces

The inspirational paper masterpieces created by the
world's finest origamists are truly stunning.
It takes years of practice to develop the dexterity
and patience to fold pieces such as David Brill's
magnificent animals or Alfredo Giunta's miniature
creations, and unarguable natural artistic skill
to be able to create such interesting
and innovative designs.

# gallery

The following pages show a range of designs by origami masters from all corners of the world, displaying a variety of materials and folding techniques. Each one a masterpiece.

## $5 Intersecting Tetrahedra

**BELOW** The original model, which measures 15cm x 15cm (6in x 6in), was designed by Tom Hull and folded from ordinary paper. Fellow American Andrew Hans decided to see whether the same model could be folded out of American dollar bills (often the proportions of the paper can make a difference, of course).

Andrew Hans, 1999

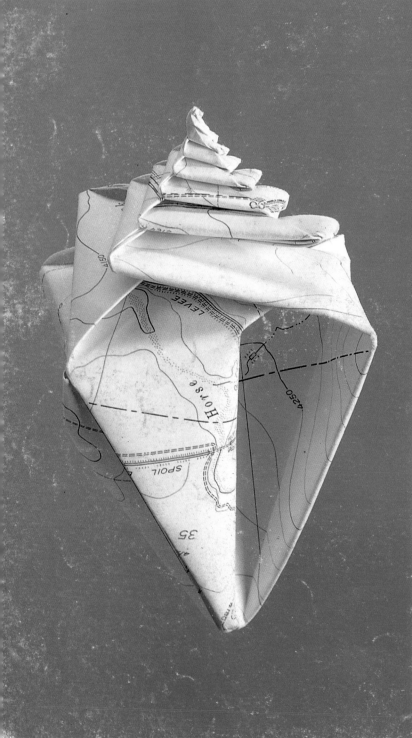

## Shell

**LEFT** Many folders enjoy the challenge of modifying an original design, either by themselves or by another creator. Here, American enthusiast Angela Baldo has produced a variation on a classic seashell design by Toshikazu Kawasaki, the principle being the same, that of a spiral twist to complete the lock. The use of a topographical map from a US Geographical survey is very striking.

Angela Baldo, 1999

## Bees and Honeycomb

RIGHT Miniature models belong to certain specialists, one of whom is Italian folder Alfredo Giunta, who has designed this multi-model tiny masterpiece; the bees incidentally are about 3.5 cm (1⅜in) long! Many of Alfredo's designs are folded from tissue foil, i.e. tissue paper that is back-coated on to either aluminium or paper-backed foil wrapping.

Alfredo Giunta, 1996

## Wolf and Cubs

LEFT The recognized master of origami is the Japanese expert Akira Yoshizawa, who has given the world many wonderful designs. Mr Yoshizawa continues to produce work of an amazing high standard, exhibiting throughout the world. He is a fine exponent of wet folding, and has developed his own special paper. This wolf and cubs is an example of his mastery.

Akira Yoshizawa, 1995

## Rose and Leaves

RIGHT Japanese folder Toshikazu Kawasaki has designed many variations on an original rose model created several years ago, which has become a classic. This example, which is 7cm (2¾in) in length, uses a typically clever collapsing twist, which sees the model formed into a tube, before the final curling of the petals produces the beautiful rose.

Toshikazu Kawasaki, 1993

## Greetings Cards

**LEFT** Often the presentation of origami, however simple, is the most important part of enjoying your art, and the making of greetings cards is something that many folders consider. Award-winning card maker Ruthanne Bessman (US) uses simple and traditional folds to produce elegant results.

Ruthanne Bessman, 1999

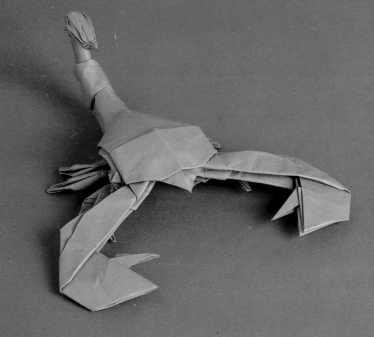

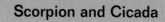

## Scorpion and Cicada

**ABOVE AND BELOW LEFT** American Robert Lang creates some of the most technically impressive models, such as a one-piece working cuckoo clock. Robert wet folds the majority of his models, like the two wonderful creatures illustrated here, which are 13–15cm (5–6 in) in length.

Robert Lang, 1987

## Mask

RIGHT French designer Eric Joisel recently devised his own particular style of producing masks, using different kinds of paper, in a seemingly free style of sculpture. Those that argue as to whether origami is an art form or not might be swayed to the former opinion by Eric's beautiful creations. He has sold many of his models to enthusiastic buyers around the world.

Eric Joisel, 1999

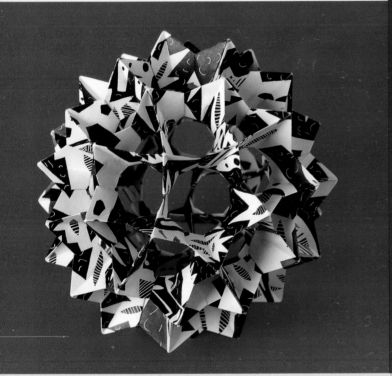

## Paper Crystals

ABOVE LEFT, ABOVE AND RIGHT Taken from a book of the same name, Paper Crystals are modular constructions made of simple units, designed by Englishman David Mitchell. David has written several books on modular folding and paper puzzles, and continues to develop new ideas within this particular type of origami.

David Mitchell, 1989 and 1995

## Boxes

**LEFT** Using intricate crease patterns and tessellations, American Chris Palmer's boxes and flowers are collapsed into a certain shape, known as a "tato", then completely unfolded, new creases added, and collapsed once more in varying stages to give beautiful symmetry and form. The smallest box is 3cm squared (1¼in) and the largest is 10 cm squared (4in).

Chris Palmer, 1996

## Rhinoceros, Elephant and Horse

**RIGHT ABOVE AND BELOW** Quite the most prolific and talented British folder has to be David Brill, who has fashioned over the years some incredible masterpieces, like this horse, which is 16cm (6¼in) long, and created from a triangular sheet of paper! It is also wet folded, like so many of David's animal designs, including this elephant and rhinoceros.

David Brill, mid 1970s

## Spring into Action

**LEFT** This action toy was designed by Welsh folder Jeff Beynon in the early nineties. There are lots of pre-creases made before the twist-collapse is performed, and it is not an easy design to reproduce accurately. One holds the model, which is 2.5cm (1in) when flat, by the centre wheel, and squeezes gently, causing the spring action and the model to extend to 17.5cm (6¾in).

Jeff Beynon, 1991

# Paper,
# Techniques
# & Base Folds

Before you begin folding the models that appear in

this book, it is essential that you first become

familiar with the properties of certain papers and

recognize the importance of folding accurately.

You will also need to acquire a firm grasp of simple

procedures and some more complex moves, such as

inside reverse folds, rabbit ears and sinks.

Once committed to memory, these specialized

techniques will give you the skills you need to

produce absolutely anything, at any level,

in origami.

# paper

Although most origami models can be folded from almost any type of paper, there are certain designs that beg for the use of specialist material, whether purely for aesthetic beauty, or because of the weight and thickness of the chosen medium. A wide variety of interesting and unusual papers can now be purchased from gift shops, stationers and specialist shops alike, or even found around the home. Enjoy experimenting with different types of paper.

## Duo paper

Paper with a different colour on the reverse side is a great asset to origami enthusiasts, as it helps provide areas of alternate colour to finished models. Available in pre-cut specialist packs, you can now find such paper in standard-size packs and even in rolls. Look out for paper that is described as 'fadeless duo' and is sold as art material.

## Specialist origami paper

Pre-cut packs of multi-coloured origami paper, available in a wide variety of sizes, colours and patterns, are not that easy to find locally. Thankfully, origami societies around the world have an excellent mailing service supplying different types and sizes of paper, as do a number of specialist suppliers. This kind of paper is fairly flimsy, yet will crease well, so it is ideal for practising your models, although you may prefer to use a different material once you have mastered a particular design.

## Textured paper

As well as patterned paper, there are also many different kinds of paper available that have a texture to the surface. This proves particularly useful when folding animals and other living creatures, as it enhances the realism of the subject. Such papers as elephant hide, Ingres and watercolour can also be ideal wet folding mediums.

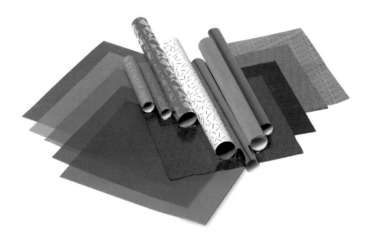

## Metallic, foil, opaque & shiny papers

These are some of the more difficult materials to work with, but if you persevere the results can look spectacular. Paper-backed foil is widely available, and this material has the property of being able to be curved and moulded. Care must be taken, however, as some foil papers, thin plastic materials and opaque paper can be quite difficult to crease well, and reversed creases can crack, whiten or even split.

## Patterned paper

Gift wrap can be wonderful paper to fold with, as it is often quite sturdy (medium weight) and nowadays there is so much choice around. Look out for musical manuscript, swirling watermark-patterned paper, wood grain appearance and abstract gold, black and silver colourings in gift shops and the larger department stores.

## Washi & other handmade paper

In specialist paper shops you can buy Japanese washi paper, which is a soft, fibred material. This and other handmade papers from around the world give lighter creases to your folding and a softer, less angular look to final models.

## Materials from around the home

Before you go searching for special or expensive paper to fold with, remember that your home may be already a great source of folding material. Copy paper, napkins, spare wallpaper, index cards, bank notes (those foreign currencies saved from holiday expeditions), and even magazines or newspapers can be used to make interesting and practical origami models.

# equipment and preparation

There are very few essential origami tools to purchase, or preparation techniques to learn. However, it is worth familiarizing yourself with tools you might need, many of which, such as scissors and rulers, are household items, and making sure that they are within reach before you begin folding.

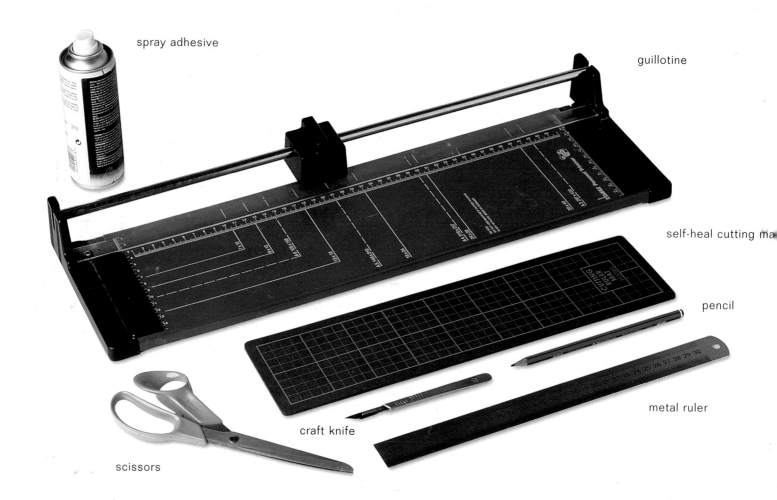

spray adhesive

guillotine

self-heal cutting ma

pencil

metal ruler

craft knife

scissors

## Equipment

Although plenty of origami models can be made with nothing more than a piece of paper and a pair of hands, there are a few pieces of equipment that are essential to a dedicated origamist. Spray adhesive is useful for sticking two sheets of different-coloured or textured paper together, but always follow the safety instructions. A guillotine is a worthwhile investment if you are practising origami on a regular basis. They come in a variety of sizes and a range of prices and have the advantage of cutting a very straight edge. A cutting knife is a very useful tool as its extremely sharp blade makes cutting through any thickness of paper simple. Always use a metal ruler when working with a craft knife and rest the paper on a self-healing cutting mat. This will not only protect the work surface, but will also prevent slipping and thus accidental cuts, as well as extending the life of the blade. A sturdy pair of paper scissors can often be just as effective as any other cutting tool, but make sure that you draw a faint, accurate pencil line on the paper before you start to cut.

## Using a guillotine

Often you will require a specific size of paper, and a guillotine is a great help here, particularly as you can align your paper with the straight measured edge to ensure that you make a cut that is at right angles to the straight edge. It is possible to cut two or three sheets at a time, but you will get a cleaner cut if you only cut one sheet at a time.

**1** Place one edge of the paper flush with the ruled edge of the guillotine.

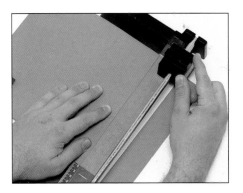

**2** Holding the paper in place with one hand, use your other hand to slide the cutting blade across it, making a clean accurate cut.

## Spray mounting

Spray mounting two sheets of paper together, back to back, is a useful technique for thickening an existing outer paper for a certain project, or for providing a chosen combination of colours. Spray mounting foil paper to tissue paper yields a material that can be shaped and moulded, curved and sculptured more easily than conventional paper, while the tissue paper gives a more realistic look to living creatures.

**2** Carefully place the reverse side of the second sheet (the side you do not wish to be visible) on top of the upturned sticky first sheet. The second sheet should ideally be slightly smaller than the first, so that a thin border will appear around the edges of this second sheet.

**4** With a craft knife and ruler, or with a guillotine, trim off the excess paper around the edges.

### SAFETY

As with all aerosols, it is important to read the instructions on the spray adhesive can and follow them closely. If possible, use the spray outside and wear a mask. Otherwise, make sure that you are in a well-ventilated area and that you have protected the surfaces around you. Newspaper and cardboard offer cheap and effective protection.

**1** Protect your worksurface with newspaper. Select two sheets of paper, and lay one face down on your spraying surface. Using spray adhesive, spray a fine mist evenly across the paper.

**3** Carefully smooth out any wrinkles or creases in the back-coated layers by running your hand over the upper surface, pressing firmly as you go.

# techniques and tips

Although you are probably keen to get started on the projects, read this section first so that you understand the standard techniques and basic procedures before you make a model. Learning how to fold your paper correctly, and familiarizing yourself with the photograph step instructions are key stages to successful models. The more you practise folding the basic techniques the more you will enjoy making origami.

## How to fold

The first golden rule is to have something smooth and flat to use as your folding surface, preferably of a larger area than the sheet of paper that you are going to fold. The second is to make all the creases in the paper, by folding in a direction away from you, taking the edge or corner nearest to you and folding bottom to top. This is simply to make the folding easier, and to give you more control over the paper than if you tried to bring the upper edge or corner towards you or by folding side to side.

Wherever possible, the photographs will follow a natural folding sequence so that you will not need to alter the position or orientation of the paper in order to fold away from you. Always make firm, sharp creases. The neater and sharper you make the creases, the better the finished model will appear. Do not hurry to finish the model. Relax, take care and enjoy what you are folding. Do not be discouraged if your first attempt ends in disappointment, because you have not been able to complete the model. If it is not as well folded as the illustration suggests, just try again.

## Ways to fold

Technically, there are only two actual ways to fold: either a valley fold, where a corner, edge or flap will remain to the front and in sight; or a mountain fold, taking a portion of the paper behind the rest of the model and out of sight. All other folds are variations of the valley and mountain folds.

### Valley fold

Fold the lower edge of the paper upward, to an arbitrary point. Hold the fold in place with one hand, and smooth out the crease with the other hand.

**2** This is a valley (or forward) fold.

### Mountain fold

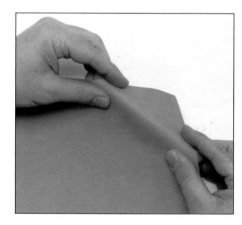

**1** With fingers and thumbs at the ends of the crease you intend to make, fold the paper behind, pinching in the fold. Here, the fold is made to a corner.

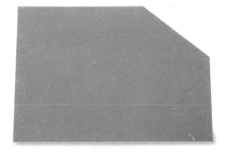

**2** Smooth out the crease. This is a mountain (or backward) fold.

## Pre-crease

Often you will fold and unfold the paper in order to leave a crease which will act as a guideline for a later definite fold. This is called a pre-crease.

## Pinch crease

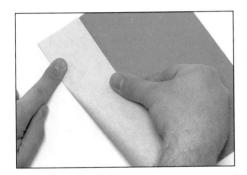

**1** Sometimes when you are making a crease, you do not actually want to crease through every layer of paper, or even all the way across the paper, but wish to make a tiny mark or short crease line to act as a guide for a later definite fold. To do this, simply apply pressure to a part of the fold.

**2** Unfold, leaving a small crease mark as your guide.

## Dividing into thirds

Often you will need to be able to fold the paper accurately into three equal parts or thirds. This procedure is a little experimental, so take your time and fold carefully.

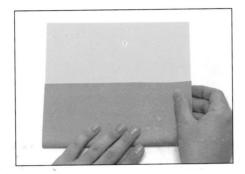

**1** Using a rectangular sheet of paper, and with the shorter sides horizontal, fold the lower edge upward, to a point which you judge to be one-third of the way down from the upper edge. Make a very soft crease.

**2** Fold the upper edge down over the section of paper folded in step 1. Make a soft crease. Unfold the paper. If you have estimated the flap in step 1 correctly, you should now have three horizontal borders of equal depth. Each outer raw edge could then be folded inward, and would meet with one of the creases made in steps 1–2. If you are slightly out in your estimation, then try again, making the initial crease slightly higher or lower than before.

## Pleat fold

This is the concertina effect produced when a flap is doubled back on itself.

**1** Make two parallel valley folds in a sheet of paper. Turn the paper over so that these horizontal creases are now mountain creases.

**2** Pinch the lower crease between fingers and thumb of each hand. Slide this crease and the paper beneath away from you, until you can lie it upon the upper crease. Flatten the model.

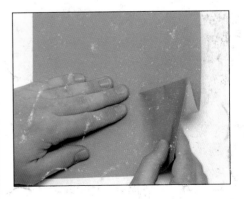

**ABOVE** The completed pleat fold.

# Special moves

There are several special moves in origami, standard techniques that are used in countless models in one form or another. Once you have learned these basic routines you will always be able to adapt your skill and knowledge to whichever project you are tackling.

## Inside reverse fold

This is one of the most common procedures, which occurs in two basic forms: tucking a flap inside the model or changing the angle of a point.

## Tucking a flap inside

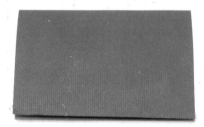

**1** Fold a rectangular sheet of paper in half and rotate the paper 180° so that the fold you have just made now runs horizontally across the top.

**2** Fold the vertical side at the right down so that it lies along the lower edge.

**3** Unfold step 2.

**4** By slightly opening out the fold made in step 1 you will see that the crease made in step 2 runs through both sides of the paper. One of the creases will appear as a valley fold, the other as a mountain fold. Both need to be mountain folds, so pinch the valley fold into a mountain fold.

**5** Pushing inwards on the spine crease that originally ran along the upper edge of the right-hand portion of the paper, allow the triangular flap to be turned inside out, as it is pushed between the outer layers of the paper.

**6** Allow the two outer corners to come back together as you flatten the paper.

**ABOVE** The completed inside reverse fold.

## Folding a point

**1** Fold a piece of paper into a Kite base (see p.38), then fold in half lengthways along the centre crease.

**2** Make an arbitrary valley fold as shown, bringing the point downwards, and changing the angle of the point.

**3** Unfold step 2.

**4** Slightly open out the two lower sloping edges at the right, that run to the point, and see how the crease made in step 2 passes through both layers of the paper, front and back. Once again, make both creases forming the V shape mountain folds (change the direction of the valley fold to a mountain fold), as you begin to push down on the spine crease running along the upper right edge.

**5** Allow the paper to turn inside out, as the spine crease of the point bends backwards on itself and is pushed down between the two outer layers.

**ABOVE** The completed inside reverse fold.

## Outside reverse fold

This move is similar to the inside reverse fold, except that the layers of paper are wrapped around the outside in order to effect the angle change.

**1** Prepare the point by folding a Kite base (see p.38), then fold this in half lengthways using the centre crease.

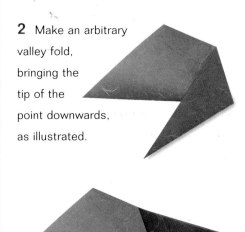

**2** Make an arbitrary valley fold, bringing the tip of the point downwards, as illustrated.

**3** Unfold step 2.

**4** Open out the two upper edges leading to the tip of the point. As with the inside reverse fold, the crease made in step 2 now passes through both layers of paper, front and back.

**5** Using the existing V shape of creases, turn the point outside on itself. The spine crease leading to the tip of the point is changed in direction from a valley fold to a mountain fold.

**6** Allow the front and rear layers to come back together as you flatten the paper.

**ABOVE** The completed outside reverse fold.

## Rabbit ear

This is where two adjacent edges are folded in simultaneously. As the two edges come together, they are squashed to form another point.

**1** Fold a square of paper in half from corner to corner. Unfold.

**2** Rotate the paper around so that the crease made in step 1 is now vertical to you, then fold the paper in half once more, corner to corner, making a second crease perpendicular to the first. Unfold.

**3** Fold the lower left sloping edge upward to lie along the horizontal centre crease.

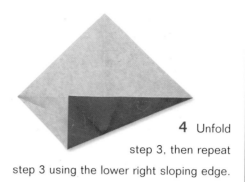

**4** Unfold step 3, then repeat step 3 using the lower right sloping edge.

**5** Unfold step 4. Simultaneously refold the lower sloping edges as folded in steps 3–4, to the centre crease.

**6** Squeeze the corner nearest to you to a point, using the vertical diagonal crease. The new point will project upwards at right angles to the rest of the model.

**RIGHT** The completed rabbit ear.

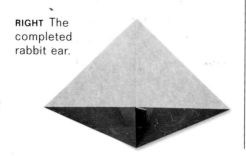

## Squash fold

This is where a flap is squashed down into a new position.

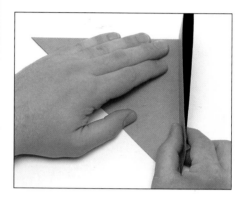

**1** Fold a square of paper in half diagonally, then in half again. Unfold the second stage and arrange so that the folded edge runs along the top. Raise the right-hand flap of the model upward on the vertical centre crease, so that it is at right angles to the folding surface.

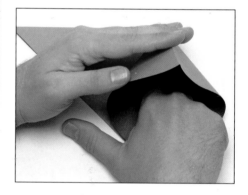

**2** Separate the two layers of the raised flap with one hand, and with your other hand squash the paper flat, bringing the spine crease of the raised flap down to lie along the vertical crease.

**RIGHT** The completed squash fold.

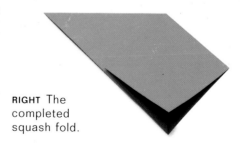

# Crimp fold

This is a useful move for adding a 3D effect or sculptured look to models.

**1** Fold a rectangular sheet of paper in half, bringing the shorter sides together. Rotate the paper around so that the shorter sides are now horizontal. Make an arbitrary valley fold in the paper, at about the halfway mark, but at an angle, so that the portion of paper that you are folding comes to rest offset to the left.

**2** Fold the upper flap back downwards on itself, making another valley crease. At the right as you look, this crease begins at the same place as the crease made in step 1, so that when you pull the paper back downward, you do so as far as you can comfortably go.

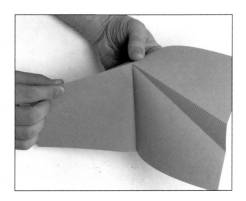

**3** Open out all the creases. You will now see that the two creases you made in steps 1–2 pass through both layers of the paper, front and back. Whether you want to make an inside or an outside crimp (see final pictures), you need to adopt the same principle as with the inside and outside reverse folds: on one side of the model the valley and mountain creases are in the opposite direction to the same creases on the other side of the paper. Opposite pairs of the same crease need to be either both valley folds, or mountain folds. You will, therefore, need to change the direction manually of both creases on one side of the paper.

**4** Step 5 completed, seen from above, showing the principal crease from step 1 restored. Take hold of the paper with each hand, at opposite ends of this folded edge.

**5** Holding the left side of the paper firmly in place, allow the right hand to bring the right portion of the paper downwards. The creases made in steps 1–2 will now allow the paper to flatten into the position shown. Both sides of the paper will appear identical. This is an outside crimp, where the crease furthest to the right is a mountain fold.

**ABOVE** The completed outside crimp fold.

**ABOVE** If the crease furthest to the right is a valley crease, then the result will be as shown. The completed inside crimp fold.

## Swivel fold

Fairly lengthy preparation is needed in order to be able to illustrate and practise this origami move.

**1** Fold the paper in half, corner to opposite corner, to pre-crease the diagonal. Unfold and arrange as a square. Fold the lower left corner and lower edge upward to lie along the diagonal crease line.

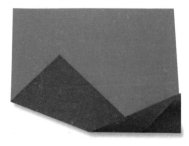

**2** Fold the lower right corner directly upwards by an arbitrary amount.

**3** Unfold step 2. Fold the left-hand edge across making a vertical crease perpendicular to the upper edge. This crease should meet with the crease made in step 2.

**4** Unfold step 3.

**5** Now, keeping the triangular flap folded in step 1 in place, refold the crease from step 2 in the underside layer only, which will cause the paper of the upper layer at the right-hand side to lift up, and not to lie flat.

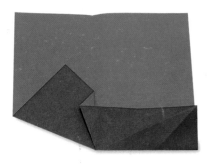

**6** The paper should naturally "crimp" across to the left, where the vertical valley crease in the upper layer of the paper pulls the excess material with it. The central area of paper then seems to "swivel" into place. Flatten the model. The completed swivel fold.

## Sink fold

This move entails a closed point to be sunk inside the model. You may need to practise this move several times before you perfect it.

**1** Prepare a Waterbomb base (see pp.40–1).

**2** Fold the top corner down by an arbitrary amount.

**3** Unfold step 2, then open the Waterbomb base out slightly, and look at the model from above.

**4** In the centre of the paper you will locate a small square, which was created by the crease made in step 2, passing through all the layers of the paper. Pinch-crease all these creases as mountain folds. Some are mountain folds already.

**5** Pushing this central square inwards on existing creases, carefully collapse the Waterbomb base once again.

**6** Flatten the paper, ensuring that there are two flaps to the left and two flaps to the right of the Waterbomb base. What was the central square has now become inverted into the model. The completed sink fold.

## Wet folding

Making origami with damp paper allows you to mould and shape the model to a greater degree than you can with dry paper. Start off with a simple model that you have folded many times before, one without pointed corners and sharp creases. The larger the square you start with, the thicker the paper you can use.

**1** To dampen the paper, use a damp sponge or absorbent cloth and carefully brush both sides of the paper until the sheet is uniformly damp. The key word is damp; not wet. Only experience can really tell you how damp the paper needs to be, but if it becomes shiny, allow it to dry slightly before proceeding.

**2** Once a crease has been made, you can use the warmth of your fingers to partially dry out that area so it will retain its shape.

**3** Continue to crease the paper while moulding the folds as required. Master-folder Robert Lang recommends using masking tape to help reinforce weak areas of the paper (such as where several creases meet). The tape can be removed when the paper is dry.

**4** Since the aim of wet folding is "animation" of the fold, you should encourage three-dimensionality wherever possible and keep non-essential creases to a minimum. A consequence is that most of your folding will have to be performed in the air.

**5** The feel and appearance of wet-folded origami is impossible to match in any other way.

# base folds

Throughout ancient Japanese origami tradition, as well as by contemporary experimentation, certain basic folds, or bases, have evolved. These are standard and easily recognizable starting points from which hundreds of different models derive. It is worth committing these to memory along with the miscellaneous tips and techniques from the preceding pages. Allow them to become familiar, enjoy folding them, and try to understand the crease patterns and formations of each of them, as they will appear in so many wonderful designs. Almost anyone can do origami, as long as they take the utmost care in following the instructions. Do not assume anything, but look closely at each photograph and text caption, until you clearly understand what you are required to do. With time and practice, you will be able to fold many of the models in this book without reading the text.

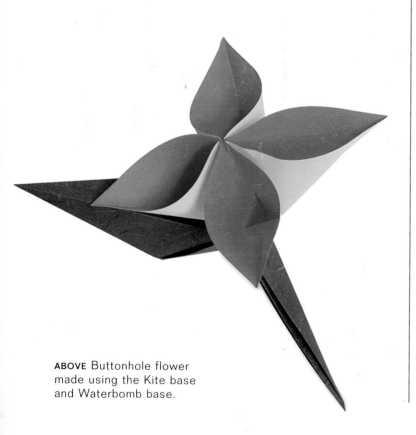

**ABOVE** Buttonhole flower made using the Kite base and Waterbomb base.

## Kite base

**1** Begin by folding a square of paper in half diagonally, bringing together two opposite corners. Unfold the paper and rotate it so that the crease you have just made is vertical to you, that is it runs from the upper corner to the lower corner, when the paper is arranged as a diamond, as shown.

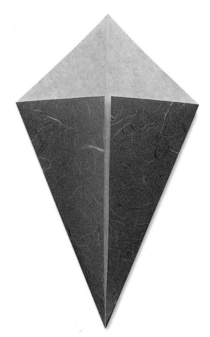

**2** Fold each of the lower sloping outer edges inward to lie along the vertical crease line made in step 1. The completed Kite base.

## Blintz fold

Deriving from a Yiddish word of Ukrainian origin, a blintz is literally a thin pancake folded to contain a cheese or other filling. Because a blintz is folded with all the outer corners to the centre, the name was taken by Gershon Legman and other 1950s paperfolders to refer to the act of folding all the four corners of the square of paper to the centre. There are two principal methods to achieve this, both shown here. The second method is best when teaching origami to children and to the blind and partially-sighted, for it is far simpler to aim for a folded edge than to try to bring the four outer corners to a point within the area of paper.

### method 1

**1** Fold a square of paper in half diagonally, bringing together opposite corners. Unfold, rotate the paper so that the crease you have just made is now vertical to you (it runs from the upper corner to the lower corner), then fold in half again, bottom to top. This will add a pre-crease perpendicular to the first crease you made. Unfold once more.

**2** Carefully fold each of the four outer corners in turn to the centre, that is where the two diagonal creases you made in step 1 intersect. There should be no overlap with any of the new corners formed, and all the raw edges should run evenly side by side to the centre. The completed Blintz fold.

### method 2

**1** Begin with the predominant colour face upwards. Arrange the paper on your folding surface so that it appears as a square, in other words, with horizontal and vertical sides. Fold the lower edge up to the upper edge, then rotate the paper 180° so that the fold you made in step 1 now runs horizontally along the upper edge.

**2** Fold the lower outer corners, single layer only, upward, so that what were the vertical raw edges now lie along the upper horizontal edge.

**3** Turn the paper over and repeat step 2 on this side of the paper.

**4** Take hold of the two independent corners at the right angle of the triangular form created in step 3, and pull apart.

**5** Lay the paper flat on your folding surface, with the blintzed flaps on top. The completed Blinz fold.

## Fish base

**1** Begin by folding the Kite base.

**2** Turn the paper over, keeping the sharper of the two points at either end of the diagonal fold at the bottom.

**3** Fold the lower sharp point up to the top, folding the model in half.

**4** Turn the paper over, keeping it arranged the same way.

**5** At the lower half of the model, you have two independent flaps. Holding down the right-hand half of the model flat to your folding surface, take hold of the loose outer corner of the flap on the left side, and pull it towards you, allowing the pocket behind to open up. As you do this, carefully begin squashing the outer left-hand edge inward, lining up the new creases that you are making with both the upper corner and the corner you have just pulled down and repositioned.

**6** Step 5 completed.

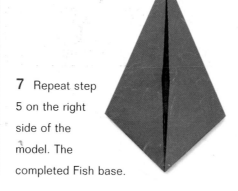

**7** Repeat step 5 on the right side of the model. The completed Fish base.

## Waterbomb base

**1** Fold a square of paper in half, bringing opposite corners together. Unfold, then rotate the paper so that the first crease is vertical to you. Fold in half corner to corner once more, adding a pre-crease that is perpendicular to the first crease. Unfold once more.

**2** Turn the paper over, and make a further pre-crease, folding the paper in half side to side, then unfold and turn back over to the original side. The diagonal creases will appear as valleys, while the remaining crease, which needs to be arranged horizontally across the paper, is a mountain.

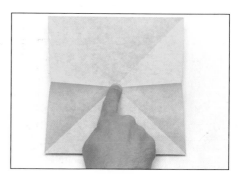

**3** With one finger, push down on the paper at the centre. The creases in the paper will flex gently, and the centre will show indications of becoming concave.

**4** Take hold of the paper between fingers and thumbs of either hand along the vertical side edges, at a point just below the horizontal crease made in step 2.

**5** Using the existing lower-diagonal creases, carefully bring the two sides in to meet, the sides flattening down to lie upon the central triangular area at the lower half of the paper.

**6** Squash the upper layer of the paper flat, so that all the creases collapse into position, forming a pyramid. The completed Waterbomb base.

## Preliminary base

**1** Using a square of paper with the predominant colour face up, fold the paper in half, bringing opposite corners together. Unfold the paper then fold the paper in half again, bringing the remaining two corners together. Unfold again, and turn the paper over.

**2** Now fold the paper in half side to side in both directions, each time folding the outer edges together and unfolding. The principle is the same as when folding the pre-creases in step 1.

**3** Refold one of the creases made in step 2. Then take hold of the paper between fingers and thumbs of either hand, placed about halfway across each side of the paper, as shown.

**4** In an upward circular motion, bring all your fingers and thumbs together simultaneously, causing all the four outer corners of the paper to meet at the top.

**5** Flatten the model. This is achieved by swinging the large flap projecting upward down to one side, whilst swivelling the flap underneath the model across to the other side. There should now be two flaps pointing to the left, and two pointing to the right.

**ABOVE** The completed Preliminary base.

## Bird base

**1** Fold a Preliminary base, and begin by arranging the paper so that the open end, where the raw edges and corners meet, lies pointing toward you. Fold the lower sloping edges of the upper layer of the paper inward to lie along the vertical centre crease.

**2** Fold the upper corner (the closed point) down over the flaps folded in step 1. Make a firm crease.

**3** Unfold steps 1–2, so that you are back with the Preliminary base.

**4** Using the crease made in step 2, lift up the single layer of paper at the lower corner, and raise it upward. The paper opens out, and this corner now comes to lie upon your folding surface.

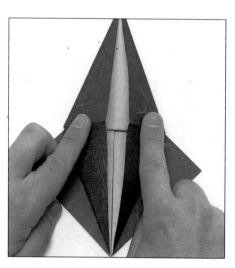

**5** Now allow the sides to be squashed inward to meet the vertical centre line. Steps 4–5 are often referred to as a petal fold.

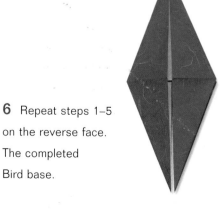

**6** Repeat steps 1–5 on the reverse face. The completed Bird base.

## Frog Base

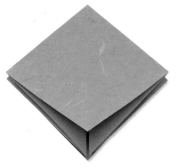

**1** Begin with a Preliminary base, and arrange so that the open end, where the raw edges and corners meet, lies pointing toward you.

**2** Using the vertical centre crease as an axis by which all the large triangular flaps can be rotated, lift up one flap at the right, so that it projects outward at right angles to the rest of the model.

**3** Separating the two layers of this flap, place one finger inside the pocket, and allow the paper to open and hollow out. With your other hand, squash the paper down, allowing the spine crease along the upper edge of this flap to come to rest along the centre line.

**4** Step 3 completed.

**5** You now have an upper section of paper resembling a kite shape. Using the vertical axis once again, fold the right half of this kite shape to the left.

**6** You can now raise a second large flap from the right, and repeat steps 3–4. Repeat steps 3–4 in the same way with the remaining two large flaps, rotating the layers as you proceed.

**7** With the squash folds from step 6 showing on the upper surface, fold the lower raw edges either side inward to lie along the vertical centre crease.

**8** Unfold step 7.

**9** We are now going to perform a petal fold similar to that of the Bird base. Carefully lift up the raw edge which cuts across the paper, connecting left and right outer corners of the model. Taking the single layer only, fold this edge upwards, making a valley crease horizontally across the paper, joining the upper extremes of the creases made in step 7. You will need to pinch this crease in manually. Allow the two outer edges to squash inward to the centre line.

**10** Carefully manipulate the paper so that this petal fold lines up evenly with the vertical centre line, where the new point should rest.

**11** Step 10 completed on one flap. Repeat steps 7–10 on the three similar faces, rotating the layers around the central vertical axis to accomplish this.

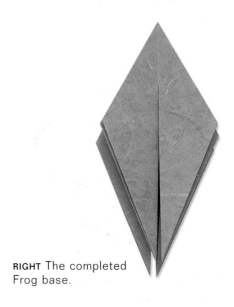

**RIGHT** The completed Frog base.

# Traditional
# Classics

Models of ancient Chinese and Japanese

origin have been popular for centuries, and are

the kind of models that non-folders can identify

with. There are decorative, practical and animal

models to make in this section, many of them

quite simple, and all of them an excellent

introduction to paperfolding.

# crane

This is a traditional design that many Japanese children learn to fold. The crane is a symbol of peace and friendship; in Japan, multiple joined cranes are made in different combinations by preparing paper in which slits are cut, dividing the square into several smaller squares. The Hiroshima memorial is annually decorated with strings of a thousand brightly coloured cranes.

Crisp, brightly coloured paper is ideal for this design.

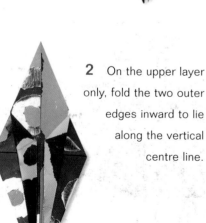

**1** Begin by folding a Bird base. The two independent points should be facing toward you.

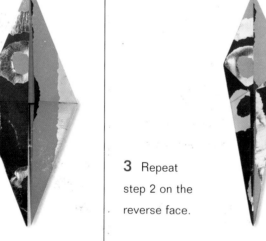

**2** On the upper layer only, fold the two outer edges inward to lie along the vertical centre line.

**3** Repeat step 2 on the reverse face.

**4** Inside reverse fold both of the sharp points into the position shown.

**5** Inside reverse fold the tip of one of the points to form the head.

**6** Take hold of each of the wings and carefully pull them apart, allowing the central point to flatten. The centre of the body will be slightly curved.

# cup

This is, perhaps, the simplest model to make, and it is easy to teach to "students" of all ages; it makes a fine children's party fold for the very young. If you intend to drink from the cup, be sure to use material which is glossy, like a foil-backed giftwrap. The predominant colour of the cup, which will be on the outside only, is determined by the colour of the square you begin with face down.

**1** Fold the paper in half diagonally.

**2** Fold the upper raw edge (single layer only) down to lie along the folded edge created in step 1.

**3** Unfold step 2.

**4** Fold the right-hand corner over so that the tip meets with the end of the crease made in step 2.

**5** Repeat this move on the left side, lining the model up symmetrically, as shown here.

**6** Fold the upper corner (single layer only) down tightly over the flaps folded in steps 4–5.

**7** Repeat on the reverse side. Open out the model along the upper folded edges to make the cup ready to use.

# lily

This is a delightful model, and one of the few flowers that can be presented without a stem, leaves or any other adornment. Its curved petals make it particularly attractive; you can use a pencil to shape them, if you wish.

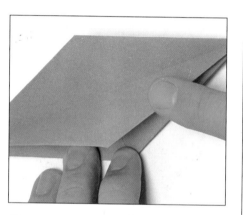

**1** Begin with the Frog base. The open points need to be at the top.

**2** Fold all four of the small central triangular flaps back on themselves to face the open points. You will have to swivel the layers of the main flaps around to expose the final two faces, to complete this step.

**3** Again swivel the layers around, so that the plain smooth faces are uppermost.

**4** Beginning at the closed end, narrow the model by folding single layer flaps into the centre. Repeat on all faces.

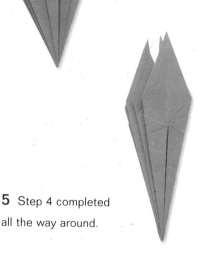

**5** Step 4 completed all the way around.

**6** Take two opposite outer "petals", and gently pull apart, allowing the model to open up. It should now be like a four-sided pyramid-shaped cone.

**7** Repeat with the two remaining opposite sides of the model, before curling the outer petals. You can use your fingers to do this, or alternatively you can roll the petals over a pencil.

# samurai helmet

A large sheet of paper will be required for this model, if you are making one to fit your head. A square from a sheet of standard-size giftwrap should make an impressive model for most small warriors. The helmet appeared in Robert Harbin's first book, *Origami 1*; this design is a simpler version.

**1** Fold the square in half diagonally; the colour then on the outside will be the predominant colour on the finished helmet.

**2** Fold both sharp points up to the right-angled corner.

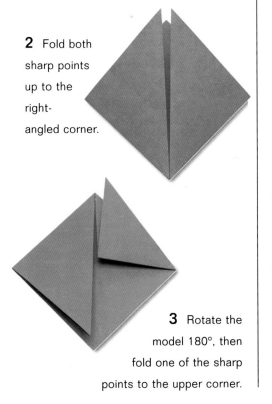

**3** Rotate the model 180°, then fold one of the sharp points to the upper corner.

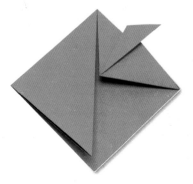

**4** Create the horn, by folding the sharp point outwards, as shown. As a guide, try folding the point so that when you have done so the upper edge rests parallel to the horizontal centre crease.

**5** Repeat step 4 on the other side. Then fold up a single layer of paper at the bottom, to a point approximately halfway between the top of the helmet and the centre line.

**6** Double over the lower folded edge, creating a band across the rim of the helmet.

**7** Flatten the model then mountain fold the remaining lower corner so that it meets the top of the helmet. The model is now ready to wear.

# kimono

The kimono is a traditional garment worn by both men and women in Japan. Japanese washi paper works wonderfully well for this design, and gives a soft material feel to your finished Kimono. Begin with paper in the proportion of approximately 1:4 (four times as long as wide). A sheet 7 x 28cm/2¾ x 11in will produce a model approximately 8cm/3¼in high: a handy size to mount on a card. Begin with the desired collar colour on top.

**1** Begin by pre-creasing along the centre line connecting the shorter sides, and also the thirds-division creases. At one end fold over a thin strip of approximately 5mm/¼in.

**2** Turn the paper over, and at the same end fold the corners to the centre line.

**3** Use the thirds division creases to concertina the paper, as shown.

**4** Take the top two layers of paper at the lower end of the model and fold the side into the centre, making a squash fold of the corner. The squash fold will be off-centre. Repeat on the other side.

**5** Lift up the outer edges of the strip folded in step 1, and allow the side section to tuck underneath it.

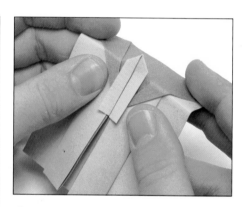

**6** Mountain fold the top edge behind as far as it will go, independently of the central strip.

**7** Mountain fold the lower layer of paper up to meet the folded edge created in the previous step. To shape the sleeves, mountain fold the lower corners behind.

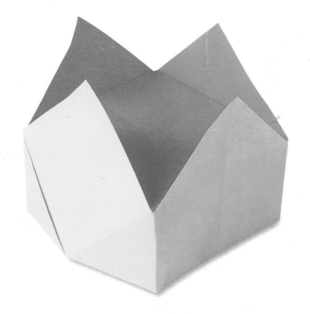

# crown

Paper hats are extremely popular. Try folding a spread of newspaper cut into a square first, so that you can gauge the size of Crown required, before proceeding to fold one from special paper. Enlarge or reduce the size accordingly.

**1** Begin with the Blintz fold. The colour you begin with uppermost is the colour for the inside of the Crown.

**2** Turn the paper over. Then fold the lower edge to the horizontal centre crease, at the same time allowing the blintzed flap from beneath to flip around to the front. Press flat.

**3** Repeat step 2 on the upper edge.

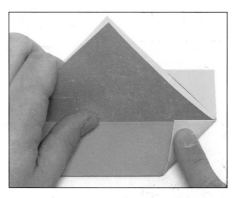

**4** Lift up the lower triangular flap, and then fold in both smaller triangled corners to the hinge crease. Repeat with the upper triangular flap.

**5** Fold the triangular flaps back down, and flatten the model, trapping the corners folded in step 4.

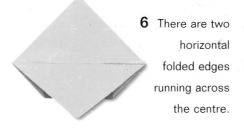

**6** There are two horizontal folded edges running across the centre.

**7** Place your fingers inside these edges, and pull apart, opening up a pocket.

**8** Turn the model over at this stage, and pinch in firm creases at the corners, so that the Crown takes on a square shape. Continue shaping the model. Adjust the four points at the top of the Crown to appear even.

# sanbo

This Japanese offering tray or stand is another traditional favourite with children, and was made popular by Robert Harbin. It can be used highly effectively as a table decoration, containing party treats and favours. Use a square of fairly sturdy paper.

**1** Begin with the Blintz fold. The outer colour at this stage will be the colour of the whole model when completed.

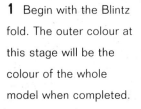

**2** Form a Preliminary base, treating the form as a regular square. The blintzed flaps need to be on the outside, so that the result will be that the Preliminary base will have raw edges running from top to bottom on the outer faces. The open points should be at the top.

**3** Place your fingers inside one of the pockets created by these raw edges, and open this area out, pulling the single upper layer of paper down towards you, hollowing out and squashing the paper flat, forming a rectangular shape.

**4** Step 3 completed on one side. Repeat on the reverse face. Flatten the model.

**5** There are two main flaps on either side of the vertical centre line. As if turning the page of a book, fold over the uppermost large flap from the right across to the left. Repeat this move on the reverse face, again folding right over to left. There should now be two main flaps per side, and the model should appear the same on each side.

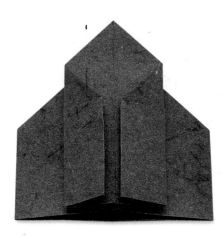

**6** Upper layer only, fold the two outer sides into the centre.

**7** Fold the top point down towards you so that it meets the lower edge. Repeat steps 6 and 7 on the reverse side.

**8** Take hold of the two "wing" flaps folded in step 7 and pull apart, opening out the Sanbo.

**9** Continue shaping the Sanbo by using the fingers to hollow it out, and pinch-form the square shape of your final model.

# waterbomb

The waterbomb is probably one of the most well-known
origami folds. The finished waterbomb is filled with water
through a hole that is formed at the top. Children love making
them and then throwing them on to the ground or having
waterbomb fights on warm summer days. Use fairly thick paper,
as too thin a material will soak up
the water too quickly.

**1** Begin with the Waterbomb base.

**2** Fold one of the lower sharp points up
to the top of the pyramid.

**3** Repeat with the three remaining
flaps, folding two points up on
each side.

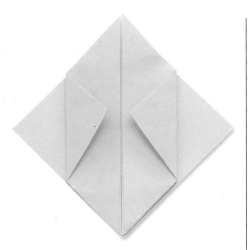

**4** Again taking one layer of paper per side, fold the two side corners into the centre.

**5** Repeat step 4 on the reverse side.

**6** Fold the loose corners back towards you, to the centre of the model.

**7** Step 6 completed. Rotate the model 180°, and flatten.

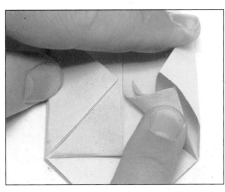

**8** If you look at the larger triangular flaps folded in steps 4 and 5, you will see that there is a pocket created by the folded sloping edges now facing you. Lifting up the larger triangular flap slightly, and pushing on the spine crease to allow the pocket to open up, fold the smaller triangular section created in the previous step over and into this pocket. This will lock the model. Press flat, and then repeat with the three remaining points.

**9** Step 8 completed.

**10** Fold and unfold the upper and lower corners to the centre of the model, making a really sharp crease in each case.

**11** Step 10 completed.

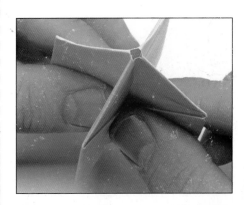

**12** Finally, separate the four main flaps of the model, making it appear three-dimensional, and hold it between fingers and thumbs with the hole facing you. Take a good breath, and, placing your lips right up to the paper, blow sharply into the hole, which should inflate the model to its cube shape. Use the hole to fill your model with water, then throw.

# peace dove

This model, by Alice Gray, has been developed from a traditional idea, and is a symbol of peace and friendship. A clever folding sequence and an economy of moves produce a simple and delightful design, so often the mark of her work. Use a square of fairly thin and crisp paper. After the first fold is made, the inside colour of the paper will not be visible, so it does not really matter what colour this is.

**1** Begin with the colour you wish the dove to be face down, and fold the paper in half, corner to corner. Then fold in half again, bringing the two sharp points together, that is, folding the paper into quarters. Arrange as shown, with the main folded edge running horizontally across the top, and the two independent corners pointing downward.

**2** Fold the sharp point at the bottom, single layer only, back across to meet the right corner.

**3** Repeat step 2 on the reverse face.

**4** Fold the new lower corner, single layer only, upward to meet the horizontal edge.

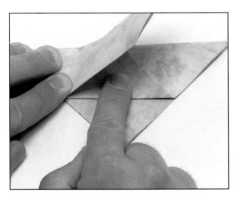

**5** Unfold step 4, and inside reverse fold this flap, using the existing crease.

**6** Repeat step 5 on the reverse face.

**7** Valley fold the closed point at the left downward. The angle is not critical, but you should have a small right-angled triangle projecting outward beyond the lower sloping edge. This will form the head of the dove.

**8** Unfold step 7, and inside reverse fold this point on existing creases.

**9** Fold the sharp point at the right, single layer only, upward, swinging the flap into position using a natural hinge crease. This will form the nearside wing.

**10** Repeat step 9 on the reverse face. Then lift up the triangular section at the right (the tail), making a sharp crease along the edge of the wing section. Raise the point so that it projects upward at right angles to the rest of the model.

**11** Symmetrically squash fold the point raised in step 10. This forms a sharp diamond shape.

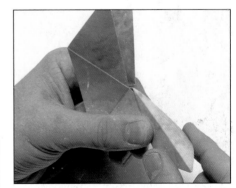

**12** Mountain fold the upper half of this diamond shape behind on the hinge crease, making the model symmetrical once again.

# sampan

This traditional design has a very clever final move: the model is turned inside out, locking the layers of paper, and producing a flat-bottomed boat which is very sturdy and right for sailing. Use a fairly large sheet of thin, crisp paper, say A3 (29 x 42cm/11½ x 16½in) cut square, as you will be making lots of folds, one on top of the other, creating quite a thickness of layers.

**1** After folding in half diagonally in both directions, to establish starter creases, Blintz fold upper and lower corners to the centre. Whichever colour these blintzed flaps now are, will be the canopy colour on the final model.

**2** Unfold step 1, and fold the same corners inward to meet the creases just made.

**3** Double over the folded edges once more, using the existing creases.

**4** Turn the paper over.

**5** Rotate the paper by 90° and repeat steps 1–3 with the remaining corners.

**6** Fold the top and bottom horizontal edges to the centre.

**7** Fold all four outer corners inward to the horizontal centre line.

**8** On the right-hand end, double over the folded edges created in step 7, narrowing them to a point.

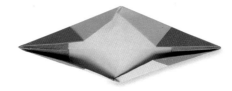

**9** Repeat step 8 on the left point. These flaps will slightly overlap the folds made in step 8. ✓

**10** Fold the outer corners top and bottom into the centre. The layers will be thick, so fold carefully and accurately.

**11** There are two folded edges that meet along the centre line. Place your fingers underneath these edges, and open the model out, gripping these flaps and the triangular sections, created in step 10, between fingers and thumbs.

**12** Turn the model over, but keep holding it as in step 11. Your thumbs should now be over the underside of the hull, just short of one canopy section.

**13** In one movement, push down with your thumbs, while using your fingers to pull the sides of the boat from underneath into a position on top, so that the model turns inside out.

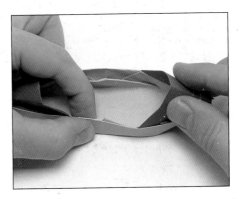

**14** Repeat step 13 at the other end of the boat. Pinch-crease and shape the hull, and the canopies, and carefully round the canopies into a gentle curve.

# masu box

This traditional box has a lid and compartment divider, which can be made using the reverse side of the paper to give a contrasting colour. The Masu Box can be used to contain all kinds of things from paper clips to jewellery. This folding method is as taught by David Brill. Paulo Bascetta designed the compartment divider. You will need three squares of fairly sturdy paper, of equal size.

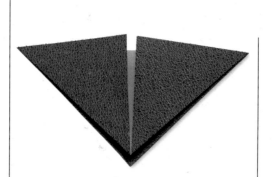

**1** To make the box, fold two opposite sides of the first square in half to meet each other, to determine the centre crease. The colour on the inside will be the colour of the completed box.

**2** Open out the paper. Rotate it around so that the crease made in step 1 is vertical to you, then fold it in half again, using the remaining edges. Rotate the paper 180° so that the crease made in step 2 now becomes the upper edge.

**3** Fold each of the lower corners upward (single layer only), so that the lower edges meet with the vertical centre crease, while the outer edges meet with the upper folded edge. Turn over and repeat on the reverse face.

**4** Open out the main crease made in step 2, then lay the paper back on your folding surface with the blintzed flaps on top, and the paper arranged as a square, with horizontals and verticals.

**5** Fold the lower edge inward to meet with the centre of the paper. Make a really sharp crease all the way across the paper.

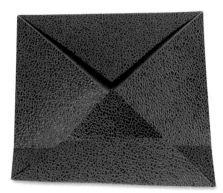

**6** Unfold step 5. Make sure that the inner blintzed corner doesn't unfold out with the rest of the paper.

**7** Rotate the paper around, repeating step 5 on the remaining three sides of the square, on each occasion folding and unfolding the paper. The photograph shows the crease pattern at this stage.

**8** Completely open out the blintzed corners at left and right.

**9** Refold the upper and lower folded edges back to the centre on creases made in step 5.

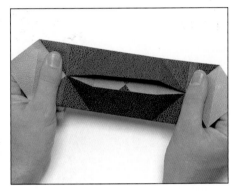

**10** Take hold of each end of the model as shown, your thumbs should rest on top of the paper, the outer edges of your index fingers beneath. If you look at each end of the model, there are two vertical creases coming down through the paper, creating a rectangular area in-between; your thumbs should be placed in-between these two creases, so that they are outside of the short diagonal folds made earlier.

**11** Lift up the two ends of the paper you are holding, allowing the inner portion of the model to become a three-dimensional box form. The two horizontal borders from step 9 will become two sides of the box, and the edges just between your thumbs will become the remaining two sides.

**12** When you release your hold, there will be two large flaps projecting outward at the sides. Turn the box around so that you are looking at the outside of the flaps, then mountain fold them inward over the edges of the box.

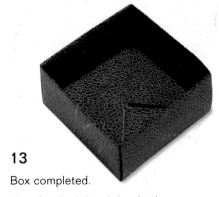

**13**
Box completed.
Now for the lid and the divider. ▶

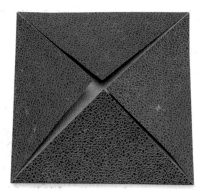

**14** To make the lid, begin with step 4 of the box.

**15** Repeat step 5, only this time do not bring the lower edge to the centre of the paper, but stop about 3mm/⅛in short, leaving the tip of the blintzed flap still in view. Repeat on the opposite edge.

**16** To check whether the lid will be a nice snug fit, raise the folded edges so that they project upwards at right angles to the base. Insert the completed Box in-between the two crease lines. The lid should fit comfortably. Repeat this step in the other direction.

**17** Finish the lid off in exactly the same way as you made the box.

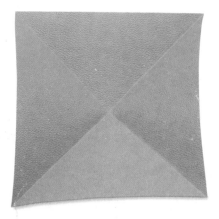

**18** Fit the completed lid to the box.

**19** If you wish to have the divider the reverse colour of the paper to the box and lid, begin with the reverse colour on top. Crease along both diagonals, folding and unfolding each time.

**20** Turn the paper over, and then fold in half side to side in both directions, again folding and unfolding each time.

**21** Add thirds-division creases horizontally.

**22** Rotate the paper. Add thirds-division creases in the other direction by folding the lower edge to meet with the intersection of the diagonal creases and the first set of thirds-division creases.

**23** Unfold. The crease pattern completed.

**24** Fold all four corners inward to touch the outer corners of the central square.

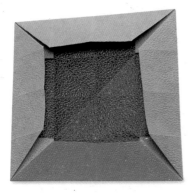

**25** Fold the outer raw edges inward.

**26** Collapse into a Waterbomb base, with all the flaps on the outside.

**27** Fold the top point of the Waterbomb base down to the lower edge.

**28** Take hold of the lower edge of the model along with the small triangle folded in step 27, and open out, separating the two outer sections. The central area of the paper will not lie flat.

**BELOW** The completed Divider will sit in the Box.

**29** There is a crease running horizontally across the paper. Mountain fold the model in half using this crease. If you place the model back on the folding surface and press down firmly, the shape of the divider will become apparent.

**30** Turn the model over, and, using fingers and thumbs, pinch-crease around all the base folds of the model, to define the creases already made.

# Animals, People & Flowers

This section includes very simple, stylized origami

as well as more complex and realistic models.

Living creatures and other animate forms offer the

greatest opportunities for free-folding and sculpture

– you do not always have to fold a particular model

exactly as shown in the illustration, try adding your

own individuality to the design by experimenting

with expression, pose and size.

# nun

This model, by Kunihiko Kasahara, makes fine use of the two colours on reverse sides of the paper. Use a sheet of fairly crisp paper, with the face and hands colour on top to begin with.

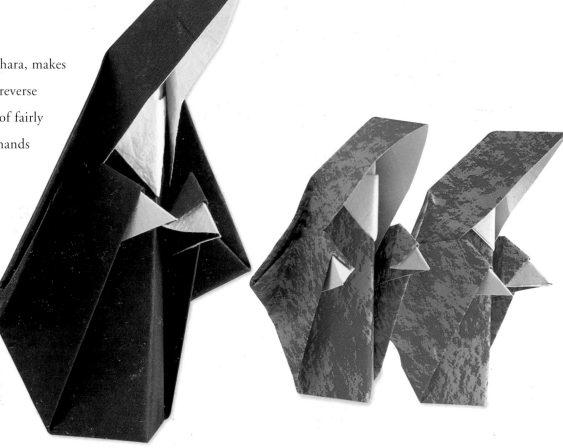

**1** Begin by folding the paper in half, corner to corner, to pre-crease one diagonal. Open out, and arrange the paper so that this crease is now vertical.

**2** Fold the lower corner up to a point a short way down from the top, and then fold this corner back down toward you, again by a small amount. These folds aren't particularly critical, so you may wish to experiment.

**3** Fold the sloping left-hand edge inward over the edge of the flap folded up in step 2.

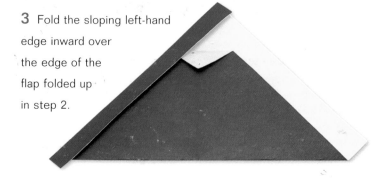

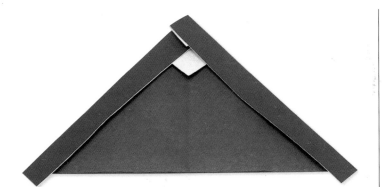

**4** Repeat step 3 with the upper right-hand edge.

**5** Pull out the hidden corner at the overlap of the flaps folded in steps 3–4.

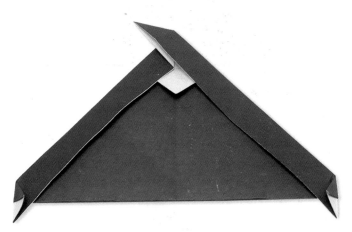

**6** Squash this corner to a point. Also fold the outer corners of the long border strips inward, to form the hands.

**7** Mountain fold the model in half using the vertical centre crease.

**8** Fold the lower flap at the right (single layer only) upward and across to the left, bringing the hand into position.

**9** Shape the nun's back by valley folding the outer right corner across, as shown.

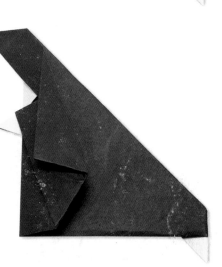

**10** After repeating steps 8–9 on the reverse face, open up the vertical centre fold made in step 7 slightly, allowing the model to stand.

# butterfly

This subject is one of the most popular to fold in origami, and there is a Japanese master by the name of Akira Yoshizawa who has folded numerous different species with many variations. For this simple design by Paul Jackson, use a square of fairly thin, crisp paper. Why not try and invent your own butterfly model, perhaps using some of the techniques and ideas used in this book?

**1** Begin with a Waterbomb base. Rotate upside down from its best-known position.

**2** Fold the lower corner up to the top edge.

**3** Valley fold the lower extreme corners by a small amount, as shown.

**4** Unfold step 3.

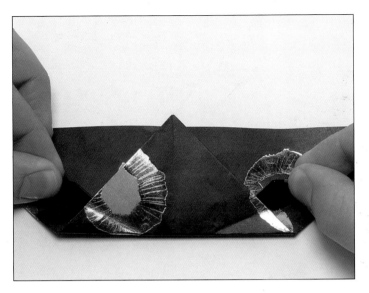

**5** Carefully refold step 3, but folding the upper single layer of paper only this time. For this you will need to slightly open out the "pocket" along the edge of the triangular flap folded in step 2.

**9** Taking the single layer only, fold the nearest front wing to you upward, on a crease that is at a slight angle to the upper edge. Repeat on the reverse face; there will be a very acute V shape formed by the wing creases, and the body will now form a central angled ridge (see the final photograph).

**6** Step 5 complete.

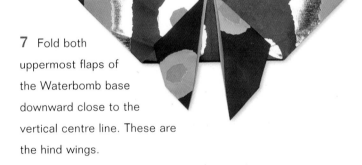

**7** Fold both uppermost flaps of the Waterbomb base downward close to the vertical centre line. These are the hind wings.

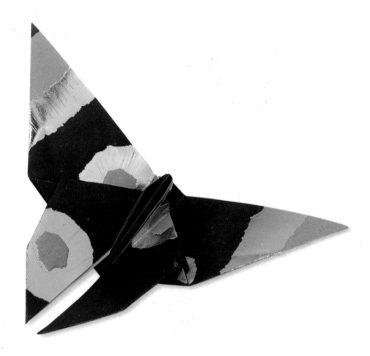

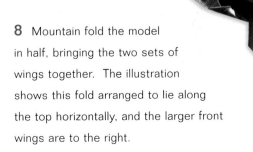

**8** Mountain fold the model in half, bringing the two sets of wings together. The illustration shows this fold arranged to lie along the top horizontally, and the larger front wings are to the right.

**10** Allow the butterfly's wings to open naturally and display as shown.

# swan

This is a simple variation on classic swan designs; however, the swivel move to define the neck and head requires practice. Begin with a square of fairly thin, crisp paper.

**1** Begin with a Fish base, arranged as shown.

**2** Fold the point at the left (both thicknesses) over to the right corner.

**3** Mountain fold the model in half along the horizontal centre crease.

**8** Step 7 completed.

**4** Hold the lower portion of the body between finger and thumb of one hand, whilst holding the neck point with finger and thumb of the other hand. Begin sliding the sharp point up and away from the body, flattening the model into a new position.

**6** The swivel. Fold the rear edge of the neck (one layer only) forward, narrowing the neck. At the same time, push up on the lower corner, bringing it into a new position, which makes the body thinner. There isn't an exact location for this crease; you will discover by a little trial and error how best to form the body and neck. The crease does not meet the tip of the neck at the point, but a little way down the rear edge. Flatten the model.

**9** Form an outside reverse fold close to the tip, to create the head.

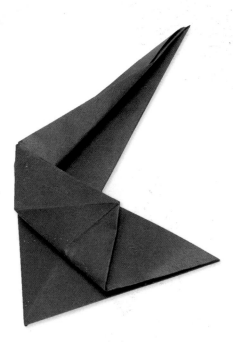

**10** Separate the tips of the beak and allow the body to open out slightly to complete the swan.

**5** Step 4 half completed.

**7** Repeat step 6 on the reverse face.

# scottie dog

This simple model uses a very clever folding sequence, whereby a flap is pulled out, forming the Scottie's head. Models like this do not have any detail, yet they produce impressive results of simplicity and elegance. This model was designed by Robert Neale. Begin with a 12cm/4½in square of crisp paper.

**1** Begin by creasing in both diagonals of the square, folding and unfolding each time. With predominant colour underneath, Blintz fold all the corners to the centre.

**2** Fold the right blintzed flap outwards, so that one-third of the flap projects outward beyond the right-hand edge. Mountain fold the tip of the left blintzed flap underneath, again by approximately a third of itself.

**3** Valley fold the model in half using the horizontal centre crease, folding the upper edge down to meet the lower edge.

**4** Fold the lower left-hand corner, single layer only, upward, on a crease which connects the upper left corner and the lower right corner, allowing the inner blintzed flap to lie released to the front.

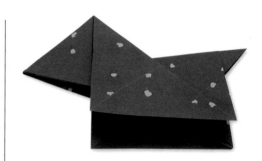

**5** Repeat step 4 on the reverse face, matching up the two flaps once folded.

**6** With your index finger, pull out the extra paper hidden inside the front of the head.

# buttonhole flower

Combining the creative talents of Alice Gray and
Paul Jackson, this simple flower is a real joy.
Fold using two squares of paper of
identical size, preferably of duo paper.
A 7–8cm/2¾–3¼in square piece
of paper is an ideal size for
a buttonhole.

**1**  Make the leaf by folding a Kite base
with the predominant colour underneath.
Rotate to the position shown.

**2**  Fold the two shorter sloping edges
into the centre line.

**3**  Rotate the paper 180°, then valley
fold the model in half along the
centre crease.

▶

**4** Turn 90° clockwise. Fold the left-hand sloping edge (single layer only) upward to lie on the horizontal folded edge.

**5** Repeat step 4 on the reverse. Then open out the wider end of the leaf, pinch-folding the upper section tightly over the diagonal fold line crossing the model. Press down firmly, so that the leaf remains three-dimensional.

**6** Step 5 seen from the reverse side. The completed leaf.

**7** To make the flower, begin by folding a Waterbomb base, the outer colour will be the outer colour of the final flower.

**8** Fold the model in half, bringing all the sharp points together.

**9** Fold the closed point inward on a crease that also meets the right-angled corner. This should produce an acutely pointed triangular section.

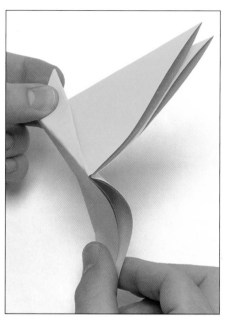

**10** Take hold of the two independent sharp points at the rear of the model, and wrap them around to the front, so that the triangular section formed in step 9 now lies between two lots of two flaps.

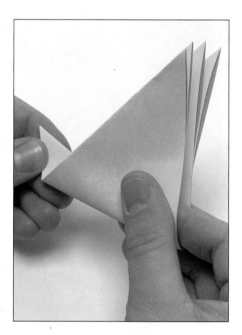

**11** Step 10 completed.

**12** Holding the small triangular point of the section formed in step 9 in one hand, allow the four large flaps to fan out, so that there is one pointing in all four N, S, E, W directions.

**13** Allowing each of the larger points to open out slightly, use the thumb of your free hand to pinch-fold the area of paper at the base of each flap in turn. At the same time, push down on the outer crease and softly flatten the paper, so that each petal remains open.

**14** The completed flower.

**15** Insert the small triangular "stem" of the flower into the pocket of the leaf, which is formed by the diagonal edge cutting across the outer face of the model. (A little glue may help to hold the flower in place.)

**ABOVE** The completed Buttonhole Flower.

# rooster

It is always a useful exercise to practise certain basic techniques. Here, a few simple inside and outside reverse folds are used to form a stylized yet recognizable creation, designed by Florence Temko. You will find that the angles of these reverse folds are often left up to you, and the final model will depend upon such choices. Begin with a square of fairly sturdy paper.

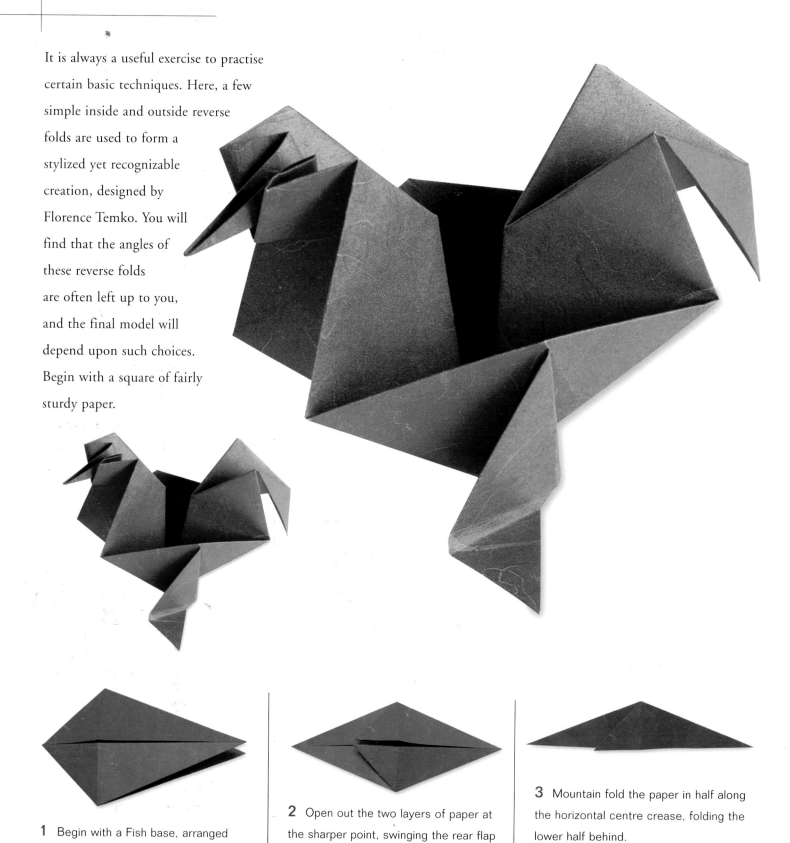

**1** Begin with a Fish base, arranged as shown.

**2** Open out the two layers of paper at the sharper point, swinging the rear flap behind and across to the left.

**3** Mountain fold the paper in half along the horizontal centre crease, folding the lower half behind.

**4** Make a preparatory valley fold with the right-hand point, bringing it into a position lying along the vertical centre line.

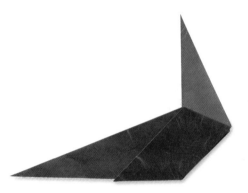

**5** Inside reverse fold this point.

**6** Repeat step 5 with the left point; this time it is difficult to pre-fold, because you risk creasing the two small triangular fins at the side. Therefore, make this fold independent of the side flaps.

**7** Inside reverse fold both points to the positions shown. The right point (the head) can rest pointing slightly higher than the one on the left (the tail), if you like.

**8** Outside reverse fold the tail. Inside reverse fold the head twice, firstly taking the point across to the left, inside the head section.

**9** Then bring the point back out again, forming the head and beak.

**10** On the side facing you, fold the small fin down at a desired angle, to form a leg.

**11** Form the foot by folding the tip of this flap back up again. When the folds are completed this will finally be brought into a position at right angles with the body, enabling the model to stand freely.

**12** Repeat steps 10–11 on the reverse face to complete the Rooster.

# human figure

Alfred Bestall, illustrator for Rupert Bear, was a keen exponent of origami, and introduced paperfolding into the stories about this little bear and all his friends from Nutwood. Take four sheets of paper, the first two squares of the same size. For the third sheet of paper (the head), trim a square of the same size in half, then fold the paper into thirds-division creases, with creases parallel to the short sides. Trim off one-third of this 2 : 1 rectangle. Use the larger of these pieces of paper to make the head, the smaller remaining piece of paper to make the hat.

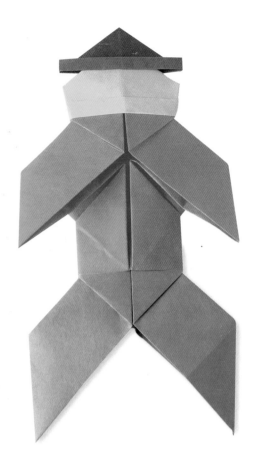

**1** Using paper the same colour on each side, fold and unfold the first square in half, corner to corner, to determine the two diagonal creases. Then Blintz fold the four corners to the centre.

**2** Turn the paper over. Arrange the paper so that it appears as a diamond shape, then fold upper and lower corners to the centre.

**3** Turn the paper over. Keeping the corners out to the left and right, fold the two lower edges upward to lie on the vertical centre line. The outer corners come to meet with the ends of the upper horizontal edge.

**4** Repeat step 3 at the top of the model, bringing the upper edges down to lie along the vertical centre line. The illustration shows the right side completed.

**5** At the right side, slide out the hidden extra paper, underneath the overlap of flaps folded in steps 3–4.

**6** Squeeze the paper to a point, and flatten downwards towards you. Repeat steps 4–6 on the left side of the model. Steps 4–6 completed.

**7** Turn the model over. At top and bottom, there are two diamond shapes, with a vertical slit pocket. On the bottom diamond, push outward on the innermost corner, allowing the paper to hollow outward, and then squash flat into a rectangle. Repeat step 7 at the top of the model.

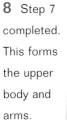 

**8** Step 7 completed. This forms the upper body and arms.

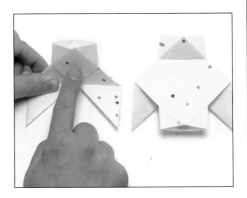

**9** For the lower body and legs, take the remaining square of paper and follow steps 1–8, making another unit identical to the upper body and arms. Fold the unit in half so that the two rectangular-shaped squash folds meet.

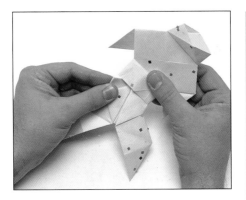

**10** Connect the two sections by inserting the rectangular shape at the upper end of the legs into the rectangular shape at the lower end of the body.

**11** With the larger of the two remaining rectangular sheets of paper, fold the paper in half, bringing the two shorter sides together. Fold in half again (into quarters), and unfold, establishing the vertical centre crease. Fold the two upper folded corners down to lie along the vertical centre line.

**12** Fold the lower edge, single layer only, upward so that it comes to rest along the lower edges of the triangular flaps. Double this strip over, then repeat on the reverse face.

**13** Slide the head onto the rectangle at the upper end of the body.

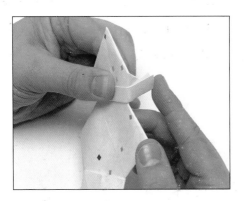

**14** Lock into place by mountain folding the outer corners of the head behind. Widen the creases slightly at the upper end to shape the face.

**15** Fold a hat from the remaining rectangle of paper, following steps 11–12. Slide the hat on to the head. Fix it with a little glue, if you wish.

# shell

Packs of standard origami paper often contain instructions for a simple, traditional model. This design was discovered on the inner sleeve of a small pack of pearlized paper, the shiny surface of which has been used to fold the model featured in the step-folds. Use a square of paper, and begin with the colour you wish to be on the outside of the shell face down.

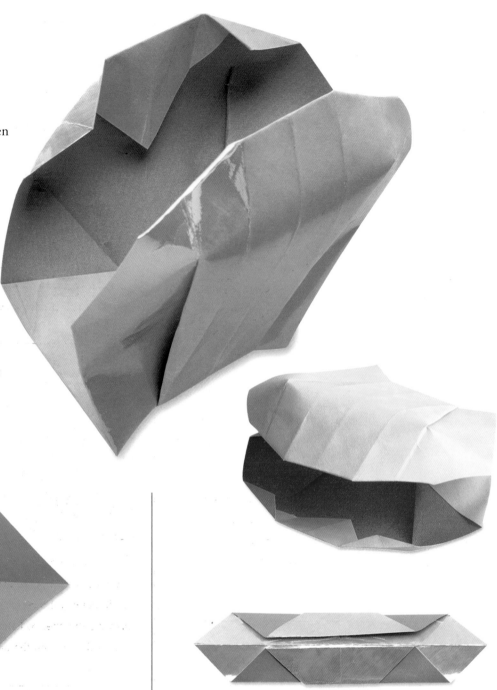

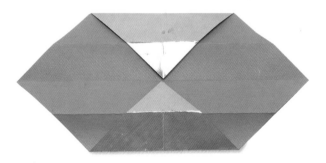

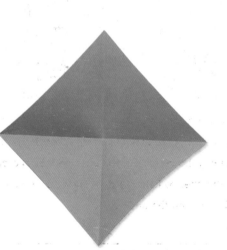

**1** Begin by folding the paper in half diagonally both ways, making these pre-creases. Fold and unfold each time.

**2** Blintz fold upper and lower corners to the centre.

**3** Turn the paper over, then fold the upper and lower edges inward to meet the horizontal centre crease.

**4** Unfold step 3, and turn the paper over.

**5** Fold the two side corners inward, the creases connecting the ends of the folds made in step 3.

**6** Pinch the paper backward at the horizontal mountain folds created in step 3. Slide the folded edge away from you, until you can bring it down to lie on the horizontal centre crease. Press flat, creasing all the way across the model. This pleats the paper horizontally.

**7** Repeat step 6 with the upper edge, then valley fold the model in half, bringing outer corners together.

**8** Holding the central section fairly tightly with your left hand, take hold of the outer edge of the model in your right hand. Pull this flap out to the side, so that the pleated area of paper created in step 6 is allowed to stretch.

**9** This new crease doesn't reach the outer edge of the shell; it will be necessary to slightly turn the model inside out on itself, curving the surface of the shell. Flatten the paper gently, allowing the shell to keep its curved shape. Repeat on the left-hand side, then on the underside.

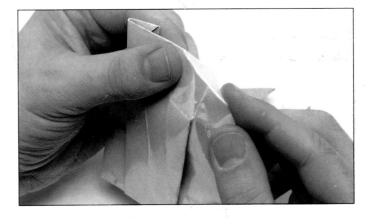

**10** Shape the final model by adding small mountain folds to the outer edges, to round off the corners.

# goldfish

Designed by Japanese folder Masamichi Noma, this creation features a wonderfully clever lock for the tail, and is a model with real character. Begin with a square of paper preferably textured on the predominant-coloured side. The colour you begin with face up provides the reverse colour for the eye.

**1** Fold and unfold the paper in half, bottom to top, to determine the horizontal centre crease. Then fold upper and lower edges to the centre line. Fold both the outer corners at the left inward to lie along the horizontal centre line.

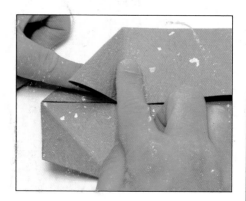

**2** Unfold these corners, then inside reverse fold them.

**3** Step 2 completed.

**4** At the right side of the model, fold both outer corners inward to lie along the horizontal centre line.

**5** Fold the right corner across to the left, until it meets the obtuse angle along the lower left edge. Pinch-crease close to the lower edge only. This will mark a point along the lower edge by which to make a later fold.

**6** Repeat step 5, folding and unfolding the right point to the obtuse angle along the upper edge. This time, pinch-crease a mark along the upper edge.

**7** Fold the left-hand point across to the right, so that the obtuse outer angles meet with the two pinch-marks made in steps 5–6. Make a vertical valley crease down the paper.

**8** Fold this point back out to the left upon itself, making a pleat in the model. The obtuse outer angles of the flap you are folding will rest upon the extreme right angles of the portion of paper beneath.

**9** Swing both loose points at the left (single layer only) across to the right on their natural hinge creases. Unfold step 4 at the right-hand end of the model.

**10** Fold each of the loose points outward to the outer edges of the model, as far as they will comfortably go.

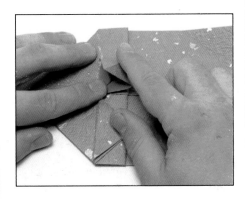

**11** Raise each of the points on the hinge crease this creates, and squash fold each one, making half Preliminary bases.

**12** Step 11 completed.

**13** Fold the inner corners of the squashed preliminary shapes outwards as far as they will comfortably go, to reveal the eye colour.

**14** Shape the top left, top right, and bottom right corners of the upper eye with tiny mountain folds. Repeat in mirror image with the lower eye.

**15** Fold the left point across to the right so that it meets the inner corners of the eyes.

▶

**16** Fold this point back outward to the left, so that approximately one-third of its length now projects beyond the folded edge beneath it.

**17** Mountain fold the tip of this point behind, tightly over the folded edge beneath it.

**18** Mountain fold the model in half along the horizontal crease line, folding the top portion down behind, so that the eyes are on the outside.

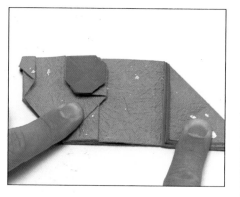

**19** Fold all the layers at the short, vertical right-hand edge down on a diagonal crease, so that they lie along the lower edge. Crease firmly.

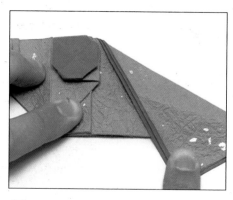

**20** Unfold step 19. Fold the upper right corner downward once more, this time on a crease that connects a point just to the side of the eye, with the lower right corner. Again fold all the layers as one.

**21** Unfold step 20, then inside reverse fold this flap on existing creases.

**22** Open out the tail section, and fold up the two loose inside corners only, using the creases made in step 19.

**23** Step 22 completed.

**24** Mountain fold the tip of the tail, upper layer only, to a point approximately halfway across the entire flap (where the vertical crease runs through the tail fins).

**25** Repeat for the other tail tip. This will be a valley fold as you look.

**26** Unfold the fold made in step 24. Also unfold the near-side flap completely (steps 21–22).

**27** Refold the near-side tail flap behind (step 24) then refold steps 21–22 on the near-side layer of paper. (This changes the sequence in which these last steps are performed.)

**28** Step 27 in progress. Note the little pleated tuck in the outer front layer of the tail section.

**29** The triangular section of paper folded inwards in step 25 has a folded edge cutting across it, which forms a very narrow pocket. As you close and flatten the model, insert the little tuck created in step 28 into this pocket. It will slide down into place.

**BELOW** The completed Goldfish.

# rabbit

Created by Edwin Corrie, this is a classic among many animal folds that he has designed. What is particularly clever is the use of duo paper, with white folded on the inside, to emerge later as the fluffy tail. The reverse side of the paper can often produce fine details, such as on animals and faces. A square of fairly thin paper works best for this model.

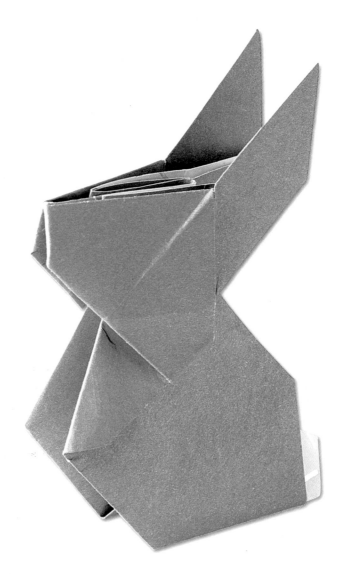

**1** With the white side of the paper on top, and having first pre-creased horizontally to find the centre line, fold opposite edges in to the middle.

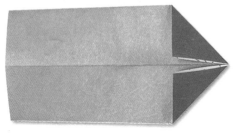

**2** Turn the paper over, and fold the two corners on the right inward to the centre crease.

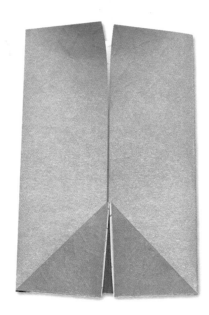

**3** Rotate the model through 90° and turn back over to the original side. Fold the point upward, on a crease that connects the two lower angles of step 2. This crease runs along the edges of the flaps folded in step 2.

**4** Holding one half of the triangle with one hand, take hold of the top corner point at the other side, and slide it outward to the side. Allow the hidden paper to slide out also, until eventually you will be able to flatten it to a point.

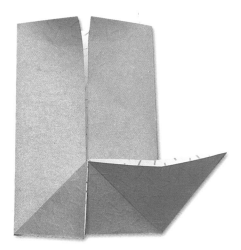

**5** Step 4 completed on one side.

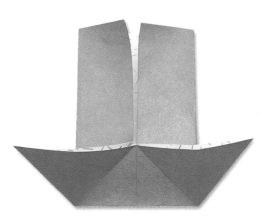

**6** Repeat step 4 on the remaining side.

**7** Fold the lower edge up, folding the lower portion in half.

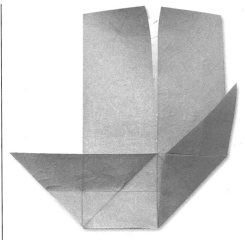

**8** Unfold step 7, then make a 45° crease with each flap, bringing the lower edge to lie along the vertical centre crease, and the sharp points to align with the vertical outer edges.

**9** Open out step 8.

**10** Taking hold of each of the sharp points, manoeuvre them back into the position shown in step 8, whilst collapsing the middle section as shown. The sharp points are folded in half as this all happens, and the inner paper collapses and swings into position. Flatten the model.

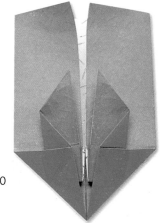

**11** Step 10 completed.

**12** Mountain fold the tip of the lower point underneath. This will form the nose; the amount you fold isn't critical. ▶

**13** Mountain fold the large section of paper behind, as far as it will comfortably go. The crease runs along the edge of the head section.

**14** Mountain fold the model in half along the vertical centre crease, and arrange as shown.

**15** Holding the head with one hand, take hold of the lower portion of the paper with the other, and pull it through, turning it inside out on itself, and making an inside reverse fold. The crease begins where the index finger of the left hand is located, that is just below the base of the ear.

**16** Flatten the model.

**17** To narrow the ears using swivel folds, look at the small triangle at the base of the ear. Open out slightly, then push forward on the spine crease, swivelling the ear into the position shown.

**18** Step 17 completed on one ear.

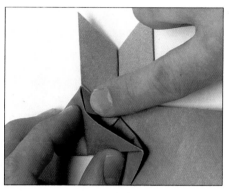

**19** Along the rear edge of the head there are two folded edges running together, which give a pocket. Open out slightly, and tuck the tiny triangle created by the swivel fold in step 17 into this pocket. Flatten the model, then repeat steps 17–19 for the other ear.

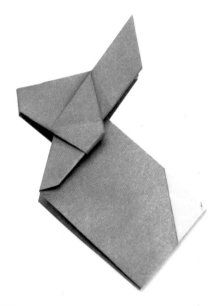

**20** At the tail, mountain fold the outer layer only inside. Repeat on the reverse. This exposes the white for the tail colour. Also shape the head, with mountain folds, taking the rear edges under.

**21** Make two inside reverse folds to finish the tail; the first takes the tail inside the model, on a crease which runs along the edges of the folds made in step 20.

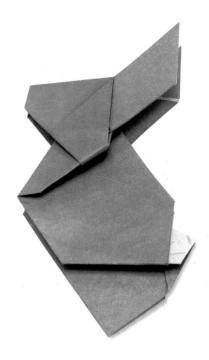

**23** Steps 21 and 22 completed.

**24** Mountain fold the upper layer of the lower portion of the paper inside, at an angle that will eventually allow the model to stand without falling over.

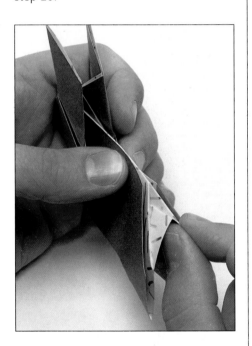

**22** The second fold brings the tail out and back into view, as shown.

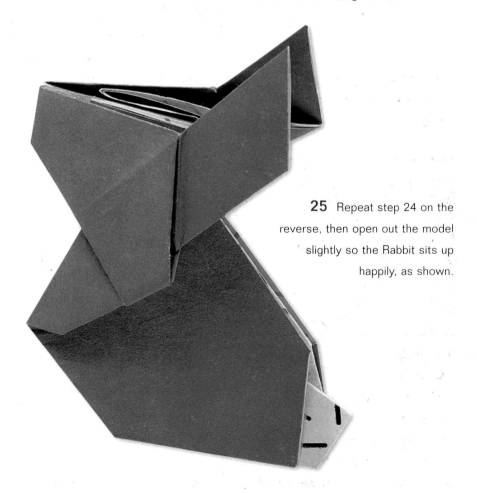

**25** Repeat step 24 on the reverse, then open out the model slightly so the Rabbit sits up happily, as shown.

# tulip and vase

Models that have been independently designed can often be put together to wonderful effect. Such as this combination of models: the Vase, created by the late Toshie Takahama; the Stem and Tulip designed by Kunihiko Kasahara. For the Vase and the Stem, use squares of equal size. For the Tulip, use a square a quarter of the size of the two other squares. Use fairly stiff paper.

**1** To make the vase begin with a Preliminary base, predominant colour outside, and with the open flaps at the top.

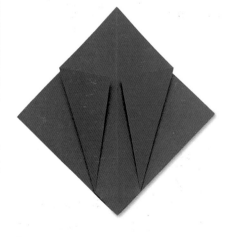

**2** Fold the side corners, one layer only each side, in towards the centre line. The creases make the angle of these folds taper in narrower at the bottom than at the top.

**3** Repeat on the reverse face.

**4** Fold the upper left-hand corner, one layer only, down to meet with the vertical centre line.

**5** Allowing the flap folded in step 4 to open up slightly, now fold the main central flap at the top down.

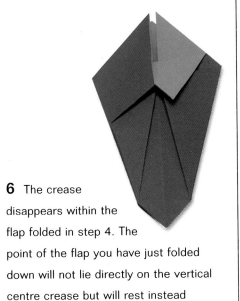

**6** The crease disappears within the flap folded in step 4. The point of the flap you have just folded down will not lie directly on the vertical centre crease but will rest instead slightly to the right.

**7** Fold over one of the main flaps from the right across to the left, using the vertical centre crease as a hinge.

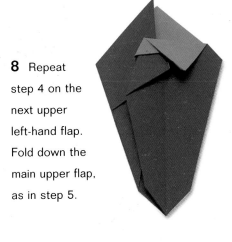

**8** Repeat step 4 on the next upper left-hand flap. Fold down the main upper flap, as in step 5.

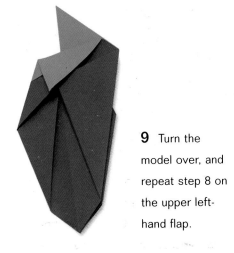

**9** Turn the model over, and repeat step 8 on the upper left-hand flap.

**10** Once again, fold the main flap from right over to the left, using the vertical centre crease.

**11** Repeat step 4 on the remaining upper left-hand corner.

▶

**12** On the right-hand side of the model, you are now back where you began. Partially unhook the folded flap from behind.

**13** Pull the final raw corner down into position.

**14** Refold, and adjust all the folds within each layer, as shown.

**15** Flatten the model. Fold the lower corner upward, on a crease that connects the outer extreme corners. Crease firmly and unfold.

**16** Open out the vase, hollowing and shaping with your fingers.

**17** To help the model to stand, use your finger and thumb to pinch-fold all four creases around the base.

**18** The completed Vase.

**19** To make the stem begin with a Kite base, with dark green the predominant colour underneath.

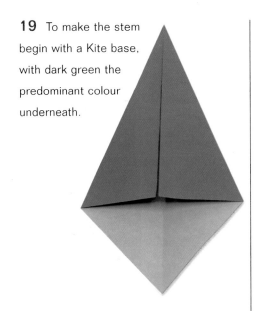

**20** Fold the lower raw edges inward to lie along the vertical centre line.

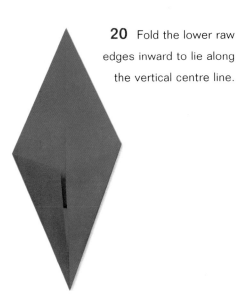

**21** At the other end of the model, narrow the stem further by folding the outer sloping edges to the centre line.

**22** Valley fold the model in half, bringing the wider flap up to rest on the sharper point.

**23** Mountain fold the model in half along the vertical centre crease, such that the sharper point will be on the inside.

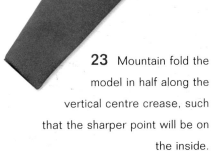

**24** Holding the outer section (the leaf) with one hand, and the sharper point (the stem) in the other, slide the stem outwards, and flatten the model so that the stem adopts a new position.

**25** The completed Stem.

**26** Place the stem into the vase.

▶

**27** To make the tulip begin with a Preliminary base, predominant colour outside, and with the open flaps at the top.

**28** Fold in the flaps at the side to lie along the centre crease. Note: the points land a short way down from the centre of the model, so that the bud is wider at the base than it is at the top.

**29** Unfold step 28. Fold in the upper edges to lie along the creases made in step 28.

**30** Refold on the creases made in step 28, doubling the flaps over.

**31** Repeat steps 28–30 on the reverse face.

**32** With scissors, snip off a tiny bit of the closed point; when the tulip is opened out this will produce a square-shaped hole, used to mount the flower on the stem. Only cut a very small piece away, for example 3mm (⅛in) for a tulip made from a 10.5cm (4⅛in) square.

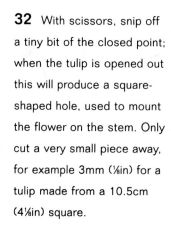

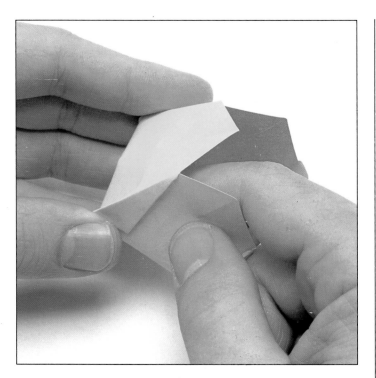

**33** Carefully open out the tulip, hollowing out at the opening, and shaping with your fingers.

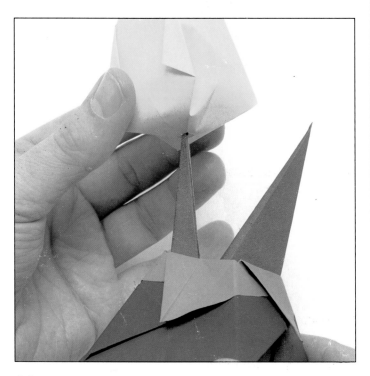

**34** Allowing the tulip to keep its shape, carefully lower the flower on to the stem. Push down gently until the tulip has gripped the stem. It should remain upright once you have released your hand.

**ABOVE** The completed tulip and vase.

# elephant

There is a group of young Japanese enthusiasts who call themselves The Tanteidan, and they tend to specialize in fairly complex folds, often with spectacular results. This elephant, though not particularly difficult to make, was designed by group member Nobuyoshi Enomoto. Sturdy grey paper works best, and a fairly large sheet is recommended, say a 21cm/8¼in square, for your first attempt.

**1** Begin with the Fish base, with the predominant colour for the model on the outside.

**2** Pull apart the two sharp points at the right side, opening the model out so that you can spread the base flat as a diamond shape. The two small triangular flaps should point to the left as you look at the model.

**3** Mountain fold the lower half of the model behind, using the horizontal centre crease.

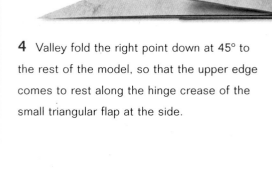

**4** Valley fold the right point down at 45° to the rest of the model, so that the upper edge comes to rest along the hinge crease of the small triangular flap at the side.

**5** Keeping the sloping outer right-hand edge in line with itself, fold this point back upwards and across, taking the tip a little further than the corner now lying beneath. This forms the hind legs, rump and tail.

**6** Fold the excess paper projecting beyond the far right corner down once more, to suggest the tail.

**7** Opening out steps 4–6, continue by now recreating these steps with outside reverse folds.

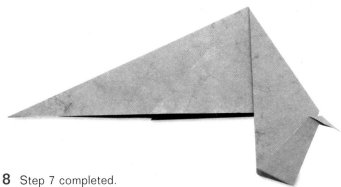

**8** Step 7 completed.

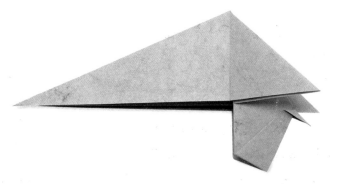

**9** Swing the small triangular side flaps, front and back, across to the right, using the natural hinge creases.

**10** Valley fold the left corner, the remaining large point, upward, as far as it will comfortably go, so that the corner beneath lies approximately halfway across this point.

**11** The model, temporarily turned over, shows the location of the crease made in step 10.

**12** Unfold step 10.

**13** Now inside reverse fold this flap using existing creases.

**14** Valley fold the large point back downward, on a crease that runs in line with the horizontal upper edge.

**15** Unfold step 14, and inside reverse fold the point down on existing creases.

**16** Step 15 completed.

**17** Locate the lower left corner close to the large point. Fold this upward to lie along the upper edge. Repeat on the reverse face.

**18** Unfold step 17, and inside reverse fold this corner into the model. You will need to push the paper in, and keep pushing until it will not go any further. A new mountain fold will form which runs all the way to the corner of what will be a newly created small triangular flap on the outside.

**19** Step 18 completed. This forms the ear.

**20** Fold down the triangular flap pointing to the right, so that the upper edge swivels to lie along the edge of the mountain fold created by the inside reverse fold in step 18. This will be the front leg.

**21** Valley fold the tip of the flap folded in step 20 upward.

**22** Unfold step 21. The small triangle created in step 21 now needs to be tucked away inside the model. For this, you will need to open out the front leg section, so that the point can be folded up inside on the pre-crease.

**23** Step 22 completed.

**24** Swing the ear across to the right on the natural hinge crease.

**25** Repeat steps 17–24 on the reverse face.

**26** Fold the large flap at the left (the head) down, carefully folding the single layer only, thus opening the head out flat. Mountain fold down the remaining half of the head section. Care needs to be taken not to force the paper too hard against the spine crease of the head, which may cause the paper to crease messily, or even tear.

**27** Valley fold the head point down at a certain angle, to create the fold required for the trunk.

**28** Unfold step 27.

**29** Inside reverse fold the trunk.

▶

**30** Narrow the trunk by making a valley fold that takes the front edge to the rear edge. The crease should not come all the way down to the end of the trunk. Repeat on the reverse face.

**33** Open out the ear slightly, in order to inside reverse fold this small triangular flap into the model. Repeat on the other ear.

**31** Make two to three more reverse folds at certain angles, to complete the folding of the trunk.

**34** Step 33 completed.

**32** Valley fold the tip of the ear forward.

**35** Valley fold the hind legs upward, so that the crease you make runs in line with the lower edge of the front legs.

**36** Unfold step 35. Turn the model upside down, and carefully open out the hind leg section. This will allow you, as with the front legs, to roll the portion of paper at the end of the hind legs inside the model on the crease made in step 35.

**38** The outer rear corner of the hind legs needs to be pushed in slightly (a contrived inside reverse fold, as the layers are really too thick by now to first make a preparatory valley fold).

**37** Step 36 in progress.

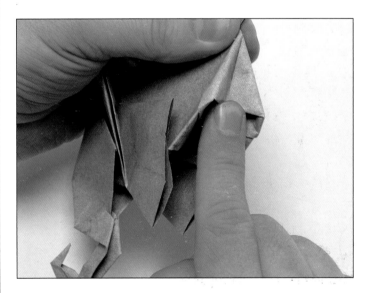

**39** Step 38 in progress.

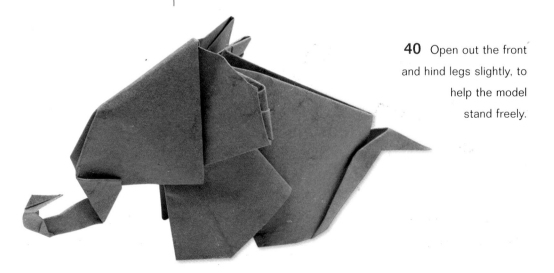

**40** Open out the front and hind legs slightly, to help the model stand freely.

# peacock

This is, perhaps, one of the more complex models in this book. For your first attempt you will need to fold extremely carefully, preferably using a large 2:1 rectangle of crisp paper. The model, a true classic, and one that looks wonderful folded from a banknote, was designed by the late Adolfo Cerceda. Unlike the majority of models in the book, a lot is left to your own initiative. Understanding the folding techniques, and your folding expertise, will affect the success of the final result. Do not attempt this model until you are totally confident with all the basic techniques and procedures.

**1** Begin with the side you wish to be the predominant colour face down. Have the paper arranged with the longest sides horizontal, then fold in half in both directions, folding and unfolding each time, to establish the central creases.

**2** Fold the two outer corners at the left-hand end to the horizontal centre line.

**3** Unfold, then fold a Waterbomb base at the same end of the paper.

**4** Raise the sharp point of the Waterbomb base furthest away from you, so that it projects upward at right angles to the rest of the model.

**5** Squash fold this point symmetrically.

**6** Fold this squashed section in half, top to bottom, using the natural hinge crease that goes through its centre.

**7** Fold the short, sloping edge of this section back upward to the horizontal fold line, so that the reverse colour disappears.

**8** Swing the entire squashed section upward on the hinge crease, then repeat step 7 on the reverse face.

**9** Unfold back to step 5. Note the creases you have made.

**10** Now petal fold the paper: take hold of the inner point of this squashed section, and fold it outward to the left, so that it meets with the extreme left corner. You will need to make this crease, although, as a guide, you actually connect the ends of the two creases made in steps 7–8.

**11** The creases made in steps 7–8 now come into play, as the sides squash inward, and line up along the horizontal centre crease. Flatten the model.

**12** Fold the point created by the petal fold back across to the right on the natural hinge crease.

▶

**13** Fold the squashed section in half away from you, bottom to top.

**14** Repeat steps 4–13 on the lower half of the model.

**15** Take hold of each of the sharp points (the legs), and separate them apart, pulling open gently as shown.

**16** Mountain fold the small central triangle up inside the model.

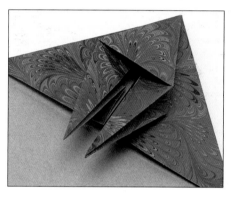

**17** Now allow the paper to collapse back again. Flatten the model.

**18** Valley fold each of the sharp points outward, making preparatory creases for the following step.

**19** Inside reverse fold both sharp points into the position shown.

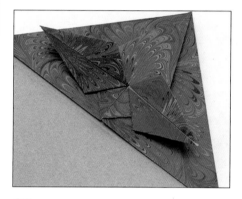

**20** Fold the lower single layer of each leg upwards, opening out to a kite shape.

**21** Narrow each leg by valley folding the outer edges to the centre crease.

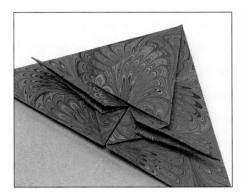

**22** Refold the legs back in half, top to bottom.

**23** Fold the remaining upper sloping edges of the Waterbomb base to the vertical centre line, making sure they tuck underneath the leg sections. You will need to lift each leg flap up slightly to allow this to be done.

**24** Pinch in a horizontal mountain crease across the model, cutting through the point where the corners of the flaps folded in step 23 meet. You will need to lift the paper up off your folding surface to do this. Unfold.

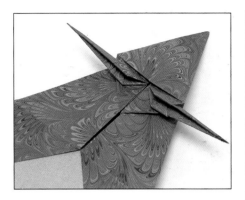

**25** Step 24 completed. This is the first tail fold.

**26** Now pinch in another crease by taking hold of the mountain fold from step 24, and sliding it away from you, until it lands upon the point at the base of the leg sections. Press down, making another horizontal crease.

**27** Allow step 26 to unfold.

**28** Fold up the lower edge to meet the crease made in step 26.

**29** Unfold, then fold the lower edge to meet the crease made in step 28. Here we are creating a concertina effect: pleating the paper this way and that, to form the tail. We do this by adding a series of valley and mountain folds to the lower end of the model.

**30** Change the crease made in step 26 from a valley to a mountain fold, then use the same process of division to drag this crease down to the line made in step 28. Crease again.

▶

**31** Add further divisions until you have at least eight equal pleats in the paper, as shown.

**32** Turn the paper over, then add additional horizontal crease lines in between all the creases already made, thus enabling you to pleat the paper into 16th divisions.

**33** Start gathering all the pleats. The first fold on the predominantly patterned side shown here is a valley fold.

**34** The pleats gathered.

**35** With the predominantly coloured side on top, unfold just the final pleat at the lower edge.

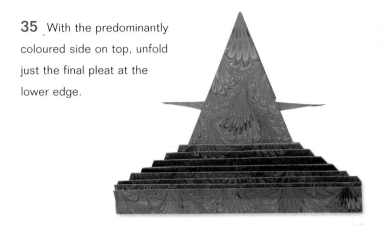

**38** Holding the pleated tail section down, squeeze the upper section to a point using the two creases made in step 37.

**36** Turn the model over.

**37** Fold the left upper sloping edge of the body section down to lie along the natural horizontal line. Unfold and repeat in the other direction. The next stage will make a rabbit ear out of the whole of the upper section of the body.

**39** At the same time, mountain fold the tail section in half, bringing both ends of the pleated area together.

**40** Turn the model over, and notice where the two edges of the unfolded lower edge from step 35 now meet. To join these without the aid of glue, fold the outer corners of these long strips together as one.

**41** Double over the whole section, and tuck in-between neighbouring pleats. Squeeze the whole tail section together firmly, to ensure that the lock holds.

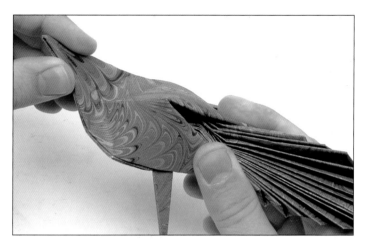

**42** Outside reverse fold the upper body.

**43** Step 42 completed.

**44** Fold the rear edge of the neck section forward, creating a swivel and a squash fold simultaneously, to shape the neck and chest.

**45** Add an outside reverse fold to create the head, and further reverse folds to suggest a beak.

**46** Inside reverse fold the legs backwards.

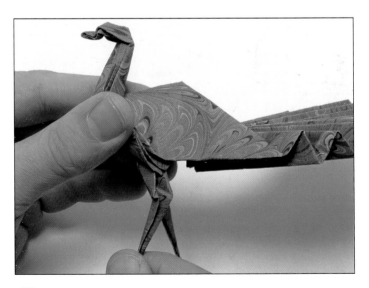

**47** Inside reverse fold the leg back into a forward position, developing the position of the upper and lower leg.

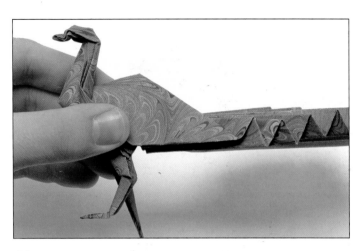

**48** Add reverse folds for the feet.

**49** The completed Peacock. The tail can rest on your folding surface.

**50** Or you can push the tail up from behind the Peacock, so that the tail feathers display.

# Toys, Games & Action Origami

Working origami is ingeniously clever, as are the origamists who devised the many and varied mechanisms for making the hundreds of models that flap, fly, spin, "talk", make a noise or have some kind of movement. There are some very simple pieces, which children will delight in, and others that take more skill and time, but which make for a climactic end to the folding sequence.

# jumping frog

Underground tickets, index cards, rail tickets and other fairly stiff material needs to be used for this model, so that you create tension and a spring in the hind legs, which you would not have if folding with conventional paper. The proportions of the rectangle used aren't too critical, neither is the colour, although green is a fairly obvious choice. A 13 x 7.5cm/5 x 3in index card works particularly well.

**1** Position the rectangle with the shorter edges horizontal. At the top end of the rectangle, form a Waterbomb base.

**2** Fold each of the sharp points upward and outward, each crease beginning from the centre line, but so that there is a gap between the head and each of the front legs when the step is completed.

**3** Fold the vertical outer edges in to lie along the centre line. This will align with the point where the legs join.

**4** Fold the lower edge upward as far as it will go comfortably (with stiff card this is as far as the inner layers will allow).

**5** Fold the upper edge back down towards you, to the lower folded edge, creating a pleat in the material, which will be the springy hind legs.

**6** The completed Jumping Frog. Make him jump by placing your index finger on his back, pressing down as you then "stroke" the card to the rear of the model. You will be surprised at how far the frog will spring.

# glider

Paper planes have always been popular and there are hundreds of designs. This simple glider, which is launched with a fairly graceful throw, is a variation using classic ideas. Use fairly sturdy paper; A5 (14.5 x 21cm/5¾ x 8¼in) being an ideal size.

**1** Fold the rectangular paper in half, bringing the two longest sides together. This establishes the centre crease. Fold two corners at one end of the model inward to lie along this crease.

**2** Turn the paper over and rotate through 90°. The outline of the model now comprises a rectangle at the top and a triangle at the bottom. Fold the lower point up so that the triangle comes to rest on top of the rectangle, the crease running along the edges of the flaps folded in step 1.

**3** Noting the distance of the height of the triangle, determine a point in your mind approximately one-third of the way down from the top point. Then fold in the lower corners to meet at the intersection of this point and the vertical centre crease. (The nose of the glider will not be sharply pointed, as in many conventional models.)

**4** To lock the two flaps folded in step 3 into place, fold the point of the inner triangle towards you, over the top of these flaps. Do not force this point to fold further than it will naturally go, or you will tear the edges of the two side flaps.

**5** Mountain fold the model in half along the centre crease, so that all the flaps and folds are on the outside. Rotate to the position shown.

**6** Fold the sloping edge along the top of the model down (single layer only) so that it lies along the lower horizontal edge. Repeat on the reverse, then open out the wings slightly before launching. From the rear, the glider should appear more like a letter Y than a letter T, with the wings raised up slightly. Hold the small triangular flap underneath the glider between thumb and finger, then launch with a forward and upward throw.

# banger

This simple design is one of the few that
the author has regularly taught whilst doing guest
slots on radio broadcasts. Try teaching someone by verbal
instruction only, and see if they can complete the model. Also try
folding it from different materials and compare the results in terms of the
noise made. You can use newspaper, glossy magazine or parcel paper to good effect.
Warning: be sure to stand clear of your folding surface when working the banger, to avoid
bruised knuckles.

**1** Fold a rectangle (A3 [29 x 42cm/11½
x 16½in], minimum) in half, bringing the
long edges together. Unfold, then fold all
four corners inward to lie along the
crease just made.

**2** Fold the model in half, bottom to top.

**3** Fold in half again,
bringing the sharp
points together.

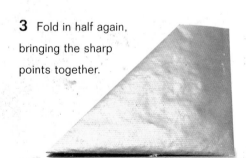

**4** Upper layer only, fold the lower
edge back on a diagonal crease
to lie along the folded edge
created in step 3.

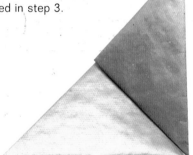

**5** Repeat on the reverse face.

## HOW TO USE

Hold the banger tightly by the corner that has the two independent sharp points.
Make sure that the longest side faces toward you. Hold high in the air, as shown,
then bring the whole model down sharply, as if cracking a whip. The inner flap
shoots out, producing a loud "bang". To reload, simply refold the banger.

# stackers

This model was designed by Michael LaFosse, and executed with amazing aplomb when he visited a convention in England organized by the British Origami Society. Try folding from standard origami paper (15cm/6in square), as it is quite thin it works well with this model. You can fold any number of stacker units, but four is recommended to start with.

**1** Fold a square of thin, crisp paper in half diagonally. Pinch-mark the centre of the lower edge, then fold the single layer at the top down to the bottom.

**2** Fold each of the sharp points inward to meet with the large triangular flap.

**3** Unfold step 2. Fold the sharp points up to the top. The right side is shown completed. Repeat with the left side.

**4** Using the mountain creases created in step 2, fold each of the sharp points backwards, and tuck in the pocket (behind the horizontal folded edge underneath).

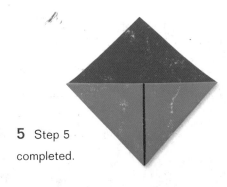

**5** Step 5 completed.

**6** Using the vertical centre crease, mountain fold the model in half and turn the model around, as shown.

**7** Fold the lower point up to meet the folded edge, one layer only. Repeat on the reverse side. The stacker should now appear "corrugated".

## HOW TO USE

Make at least three more units, then stack them on top of each other and lay them in the palm of your hand, with the two-coloured side uppermost. The thicker, heavier end should face towards your fingertips and all the units should face the same way. Throw the pile of stackers high into the air. They will separate and fly off in different directions.

# barking dog

This design is by Ulrike Krallmann-Wenzel. How clever to be able to add a couple of creases to what is a standard base, open out the paper completely, re-collapse it, and have a wonderful action toy. Begin with a square of crisp paper, preferably duo.

**1** Fold a Preliminary base, with the opening facing you. Fold in both layers on the left-hand side so that they rest at a point a little below the centre.

**2** Fold the closed point down, on a crease which connects the right-hand corner, and the upper end of the flaps folded in step 2. Make firm creases.

**3** Open the paper out enough to be able to see the crease pattern formed. Using the photograph as a guide, change the direction of certain creases, so that you can collapse the paper into the form shown. See how particular creases on either side of the model need to be made to face the same direction.

**4** Steps 3 and 4 completed.

**5** Turn the tip of the nose outside on itself, which makes use of the reverse colour of your paper.

## HOW TO USE

To make the dog "bark", hold him by the chest with one hand, the tail with the other (you will need to supply the noise yourself). Gently pull the tail, allowing the paper to open and collapse back. The head will raise in excitement.

# zoomerang

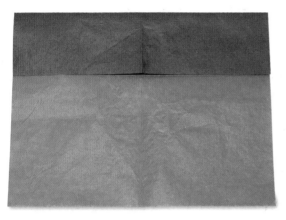

Sanny Ang, an Australian paperfolder, visited England a while back, and amazed crowds by demonstrating how to throw this model away from you in such a way, that it can be "trained" to land on your head on its way back. Use a square of thin, crisp paper for best results, and practise adjusting the proportions of the model's folds to give the effect you desire.

**1** After pre-creasing the horizontal and vertical halfway lines of a square of paper, fold the upper edge down to the centre.

**2** Valley fold the model in half side to side, left to right.

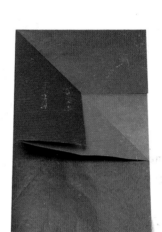

**3** Fold back the upper right corner (single layer only) to lie along the left-hand vertical edge.

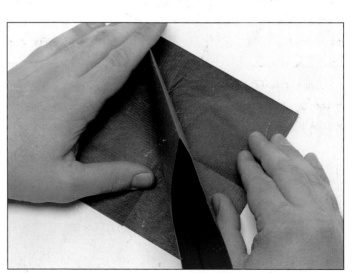

**4** Repeat step 3 on the reverse face. Then open up the model from below, swinging the larger flap in between layers upward, so that it rests perpendicular to your folding surface. The side flaps should arrange themselves as shown.

▶

**5** Open out and separate the layers of this 90° section, and make a squash fold, bringing the folded edge down to the baseline, forming a large triangle. Turn the model over.

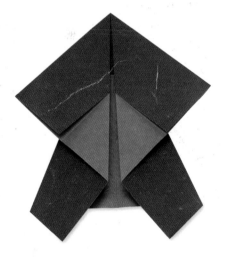

**6** Step 5 completed.

**7** Fold down the upper corner so that if you were to imagine a line drawn horizontally across the reverse-coloured central diamond, the tip of the corner would meet this line.

**8** Fold the same corner back up on itself.

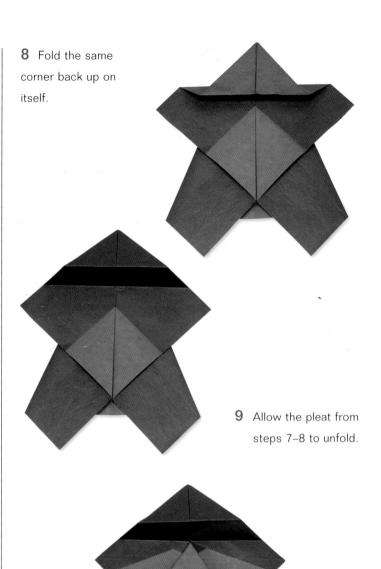

**9** Allow the pleat from steps 7–8 to unfold.

**10** Fold out the lower flaps, on creases connecting the lower extreme right and left corners with the vertical centre line, where it intersects with the crease made in step 7. Sharply pre-crease, then unfold the flaps.

**11** Reform the pleat from steps 7–8. Mountain fold the model in half along the centre crease.

**12** Rotating the paper around slightly, and folding one layer only at a time, fold the wing section across the model. The crease begins at the corner of the pleat, and brings the outer edge of the wing approximately to the mountain-folded edge created in step 11. The location of this crease isn't critical, so experiment with various widths for the undercarriage of the Zoomerang. Unfold these pre-creases.

**15** Finally valley fold up the remaining wing, to lie upon the other to complete the Zoomerang.

**13** Carefully refold step 10, the large flaps folding outward on existing creases.

## HOW TO USE

The finished model will have a thin strip running down the length of the undercarriage. Take hold of this section, fairly close to the front of the Zoomerang. Hold the Zoomerang straight out in front of you, perpendicular to the ground, and with the nose uppermost, as shown. Raise your arm quickly, launching the model into the air. You can expect it to loop-the-loop, and return. You may need to make certain adjustments to the wings, and try different angles within the folding sequence, to achieve the desired results.
Keep practising.

**14** Pinching the vertical centre line as a mountain fold, slide away from you and lie this folded edge on to the crease line made in step 12.

# tumblewing

Kosho Uchiyama has designed this variation on a popular theme: a model which can be held high in the air, then dropped, causing it to spin as it comes to land. Use a square of thin, crisp paper, as there are quite a few layers building up in the design as you progress through the latter stages.

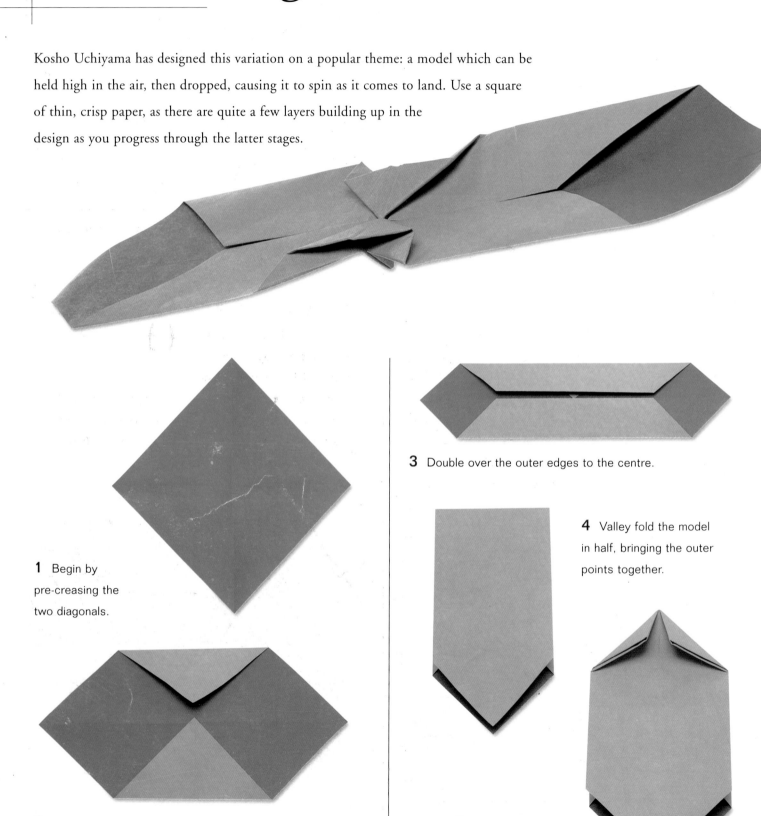

**1** Begin by pre-creasing the two diagonals.

**2** Blintz fold the upper and lower corners to the centre.

**3** Double over the outer edges to the centre.

**4** Valley fold the model in half, bringing the outer points together.

**5** At the top fold the right-angled corners to the centre crease.

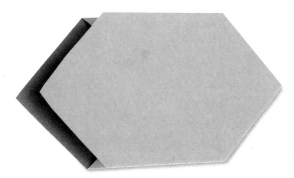

**6** Unfold step 5, then inside reverse fold these corners into the model.

**7** Fold the top corner (the closed point formed by the reverse folds previously made) down, to arrive at a point level with the two upper angles.

**8** Leaving the small corner from step 7 firmly folded, open out the central valley fold once more, so that once again you have a long strip. The central area will not lie flat.

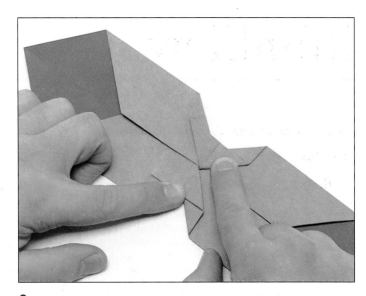

**9** Squash the central flaps down symmetrically, forming a kind of bow-tie shape, to complete the Tumblewing.

## HOW TO USE

Turn the model over, and raise the small triangular flap so that it projects upward at right angles to the rest of the model. Hold this point between your first two fingers, and then raise your arm high in the air, at approximately a 45° angle. Allow the model to slip from your fingers, and watch the effect as it gently spins away from you to the floor.

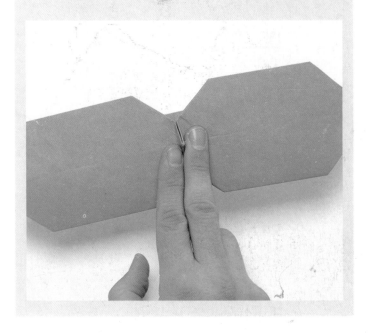

# nodding dog

Paul Jackson devised this simple origami version of the classic car rear-window toy. As ever, it is important to fold with good, accurate creases, particularly as the action depends upon the sharpness of the folding. Use two squares of similarly coloured paper, preferably with a reverse colour. Begin by making the body, having the colour you wish to be predominant when you have finished the model face down.

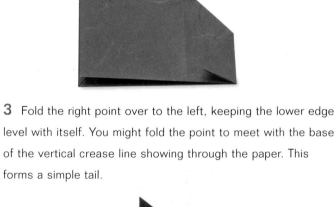

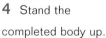

1  For the body, fold and unfold the paper in half diagonally in both directions. Blintz fold all four corners to the centre.

2  Fold the model in half diagonally.

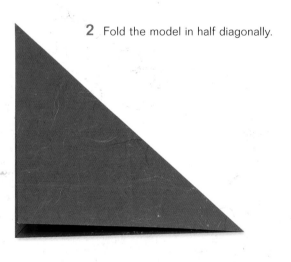

3  Fold the right point over to the left, keeping the lower edge level with itself. You might fold the point to meet with the base of the vertical crease line showing through the paper. This forms a simple tail.

4  Stand the completed body up.

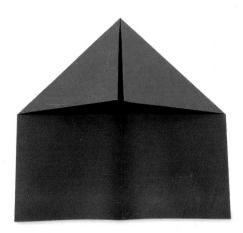

**5** To make the head begin with the paper as a square, that is with horizontals and verticals, predominant colour face down, and fold in half side to side to fold in the vertical centre crease. Then fold the upper corners down to lie on the centre line.

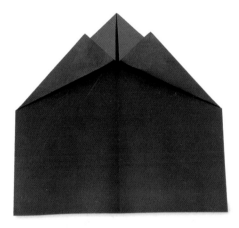

**6** Fold each of the triangular flaps upward and outward, so that the horizontal edges come to lie along the sloping edges.

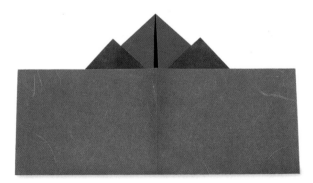

**7** The two triangular flaps created in step 2 meet along the vertical centre line. Fold up the lower edge to a point a few millimetres/1/16–1/4in above where they meet. This will form the eyes.

**8** Fold the top point down to form the nose. The fold is about a third of the distance from the tip to the long horizontal edge.

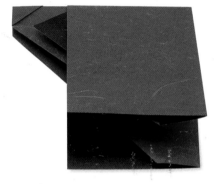

**9** Mountain fold the model in half along the vertical centre line, so that the eyes remain on the outside.

## HOW TO USE

Balance the head onto the sharp point at the top of the body. This point should go right up the centre of the head, and not caught in the side flaps. Gently push down on the nose with one finger, and the head will nod up and down.

# magic star/frisbee

For this classic Bob Neale model, you will need eight small squares of paper, preferably smooth to the touch (rough, textured paper will spoil the easy action of the model). Repeat all steps on each sheet of paper.

**1** Fold the paper, in half side to side, pattern-/colour-side face down.

**2** With the fold made in step 1 towards you, fold the lower right-hand corner up at 45° so that it lies along the upper raw edges, and makes a sharp point at the right-hand side.

**3** Open out step 2, and inside reverse fold this section of the paper.

**4** Open out the model slightly from above. At the other end, fold the remaining corners inside on 45° creases, to meet the folded edge. Collapse the paper flat once more.

**5** Place the original unit on a table lying vertically. Make seven more units and arrange them on a table as shown.

**6** Take any second unit, and slide it into position within the original unit, as shown, the second unit sliding between the open points of the first. Hold it in place.

**7** Lock the units together by folding both of the excess tips of the open points of the first unit tightly over the edges of the second (the facing flap is mountain-folded, the rear flap valley-folded, as you look).

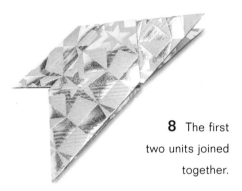

**8** The first two units joined together.

**9** Continue joining the remaining units clockwise. As shown, when you have joined six units, you seem to come to a point where you can go no further, and the ring looks almost complete. At this point you must carefully arrange the final two units so that, as you join them in sequence, you are also allowing unit one to be joined to unit eight.

## HOW TO USE

The Magic Star completed. To convert to the Frisbee, take hold of any two opposite segments of the central octagon shape...,

... and gently slide outward, so that a hole begins to appear at the centre.

Then take hold of two different segments, and again slide outward, so that the hole opens up even more.

Keep rotating and repeating this process, until you have your Frisbee. To return to the Magic Star, simply repeat the opening process in reverse.

# pecking crow

Some models contain a clever little move in the folding sequence that makes the design memorable. So it is with this action toy created by Makoto Yamaguchi, where folds are made through two layers of paper, so that when the layers are separated the folds are kept in place. Use a square of duo-coloured paper, with the predominant colour face down.

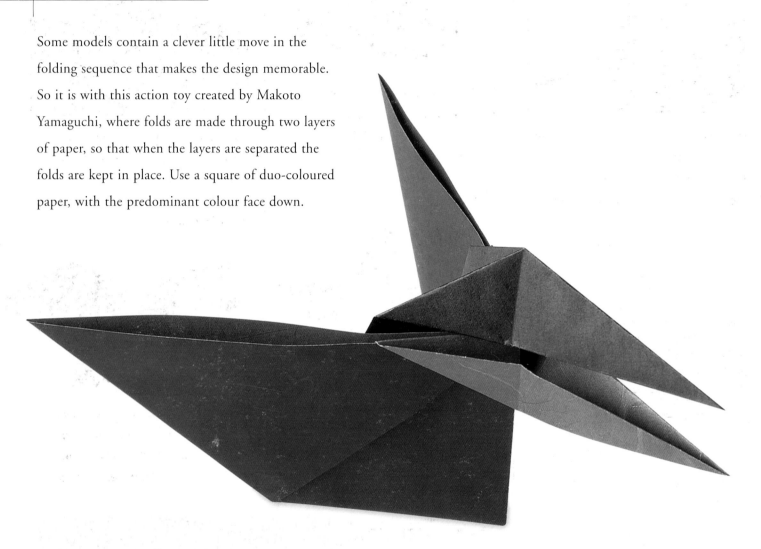

**1** Begin by folding the paper in half diagonally. Then fold into quarters, merely to establish the vertical centre line as shown. Unfold.

**2** Fold each of the double raw edges down to lie along the vertical centre crease.

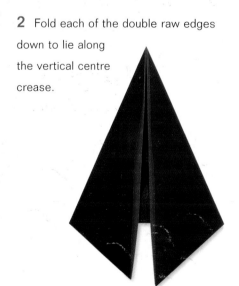

**3** Fold each of the pointed flaps outward as far as they will go, so that the creases connect with the lower extreme corners. Their upper edges will be parallel to the lower horizontal edge.

**4** Open out the section of paper at the top slightly, and you will observe one layer inside the other. Pull out the single upper layer, separating it from the outer layer wrapped around it.

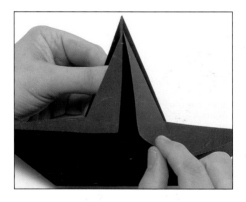

**5** Continue pulling the inner flap completely out.

**6** Flatten the model.

**7** Fold the upper corner (single layer only) down towards you as far as it will comfortably go.

**8** Fold this point across to the right, so that the lower left edge comes up to lie along the central horizontal edge. Make a crease.

**9** Unfold step 8, and repeat it in the other direction. Unfold once more.

**10** Form a rabbit ear of the lower point, squeezing the paper together at the point, and allowing it to remain projecting upward at right angles to the rest of the model.

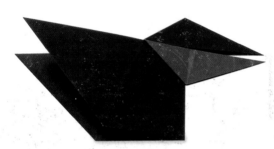

**11** Turn the model over and repeat steps 7–10. Then mountain fold the model in half using the vertical centre crease. The completed Pecking Crow.

## HOW TO USE

To make the beak open you pull the wings slightly apart.

# flapping bird

There are a great many flapping birds in origami, designed by folders worldwide, but my all-time favourite is this Paul Jackson variation on an original model by Sam Randlett. It has a wonderfully clean action that never fails to work; although there are a couple of moves that are quite tricky to understand. Use a square of crisp paper.

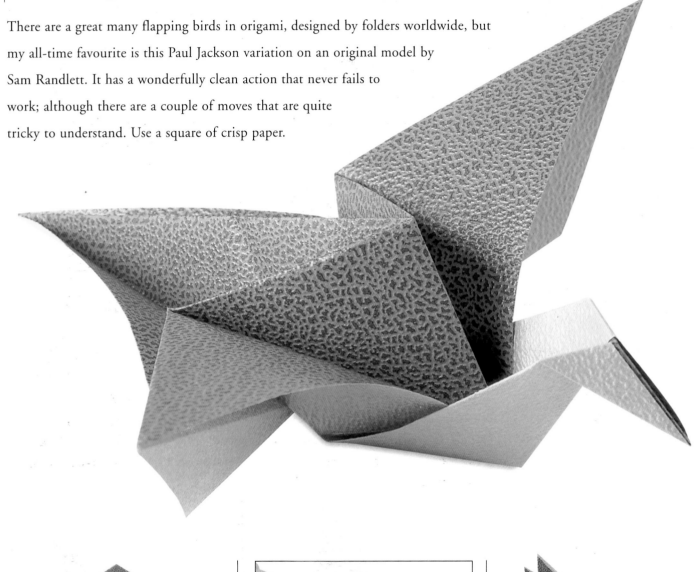

**1** Begin with a Waterbomb base. The final model has a fairly equal colour ratio, so it never seems to matter which side of the paper faces you to begin with.

**2** There are two sharp points on each side of the Waterbomb base. Fold the top point only on the right-hand side across to the left.

**3** Fold the lower horizontal edge up to lie on the upper-right sloping edge. Make a really firm crease.

**4** Unfold step 3.

**5** Folding the single layer only, take hold of the uppermost point at the left, and make a repeat fold of step 3, using the same crease. As the flap comes to rest, you have to make a swivel-squash adjustment with excess paper between layers, so that the model will lie flat once more.

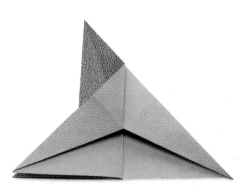

**6** Step 5 completed.

**7** Turn the model over, and arrange it so that the crease made in step 3 rises from left to right.

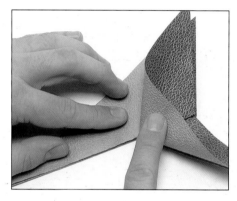

**8** Repeat step 5 on this side, folding the single point at the right up to lie on the upper left sloping edge, matching the two wings together, and making a similar swivel-squash adjustment to that in step 5.

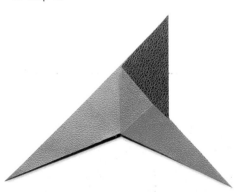

**9** Step 8 completed.

**10** Make a valley fold in the left-hand point, so that the crease runs in line with the lower edge of the right-hand point.

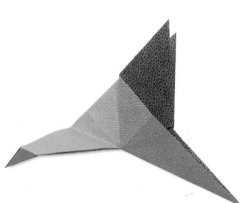

**11** Change the angle of the left-hand point, by making another valley fold at the tip. These last two steps form the neck and head respectively.

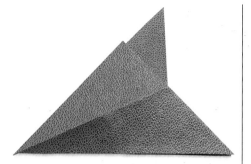

**12** Open out steps 10–11.

▶

**13** Turn the model over, so that you are now looking at the underside of the bird. Open out the pocket between the folded-edged layers of each of the sharp points, and hold with the point that has the creases made in steps 10–11 facing away from you.

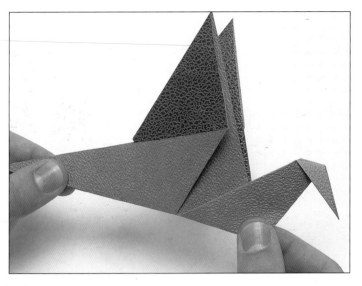

**16** Flatten the model.

**14** Using the larger V shape of existing creases, outside reverse fold the neck into position. The point will be turned outside on itself.

**RIGHT** The completed Flapping Bird.

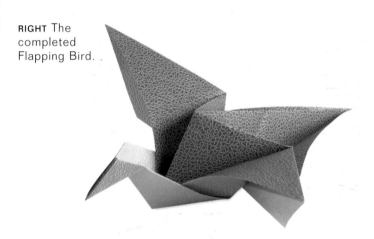

**15** Using the V shape of existing creases at the tip of the neck point, make a further outside reverse fold to form the head.

## HOW TO USE

Hold the chest of the bird with one hand, and the tail with the other. Pull the tail gently allowing the model to open slightly and collapse again, for a wonderful flapping action.

# talking frog

Created by the folder Teruo Tsuji, this delightful model uses a common mechanism to produce a talking action. Use a large sheet (say, A3 [29 x 42cm/11½ x 16½in] cut square) of thin paper, as the layers do tend to become quite thick as you proceed through the folding sequence. Ideally, have green as the reverse colour, which should begin face down.

**1** Fold the paper in half diagonally.

**2** Fold the sharp points up to the top.

**3** Fold in half diagonally again, this time only pinch-folding to find the centre of the model. ▶

**4** Fold the sharp points down to the centre.

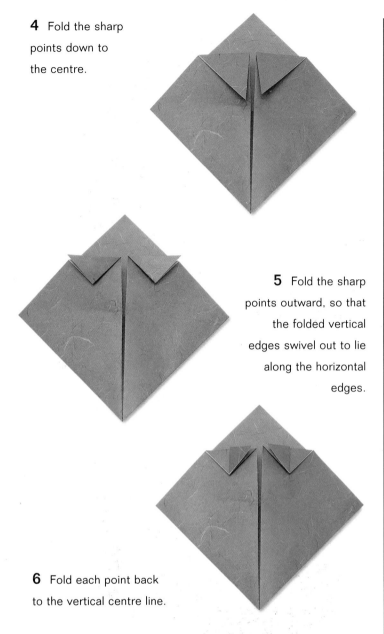

**5** Fold the sharp points outward, so that the folded vertical edges swivel out to lie along the horizontal edges.

**6** Fold each point back to the vertical centre line.

**7** Raise points on the natural hinge creases, so that they are at right angles to the rest of the model. Squash fold each point, forming half-Preliminary bases.

**8** Step 7 complete on both sides.

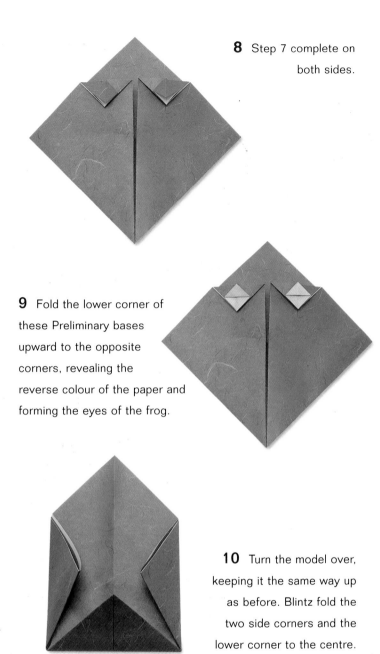

**9** Fold the lower corner of these Preliminary bases upward to the opposite corners, revealing the reverse colour of the paper and forming the eyes of the frog.

**10** Turn the model over, keeping it the same way up as before. Blintz fold the two side corners and the lower corner to the centre.

**11** Make a rabbit ear of the lower blintzed flap, while folding the side corners back outward to their respective outside edges.

**12** Carefully pinch-fold the upper portions of the model over the edges of the side flaps folded in step 11, creasing hard between the outer edges and the vertical centre line.

**13** Step 12 completed on both sides.

**14** Mountain fold the model in half, so that the two sides rest at approximate right angles with each other. While holding the model in this position with one hand, use the other hand to take hold of the single layer of paper at the top, and gently pull it downward, making a soft new crease, and forming a diamond shape in the frog's mouth.

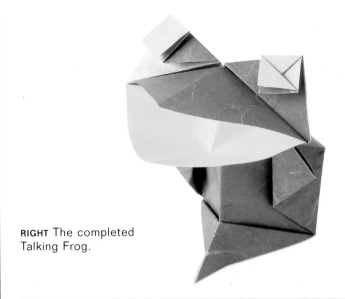

**RIGHT** The completed Talking Frog.

## HOW TO USE

Allow the paper to relax for the mouth to open. Flex the vertical mountain crease, up the centre of the body back, to make the mouth close.

# catapult and basketball hoop

These two models combine to wonderful effect, the Catapult designed by Robert Lang, and the Basketball Hoop, a traditional playground fold. For the Catapult, use a square of fairly crisp paper, cut from a sheet of A4 (21 x 29cm/8¼ x 11½in). For the Basketball Hoop use a sheet of reasonably sturdy A4 paper.

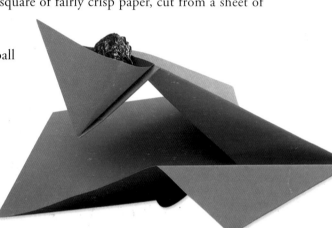

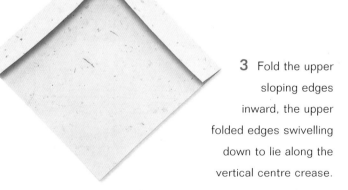

**1** To make the Catapult, after folding the square in half to locate the diagonal crease, unfold, then pinch in the centre mark of the remaining diagonal.

**2** Unfold step 1, then fold the upper corner down by approximately a third of the distance between itself and the centre pinch.

**3** Fold the upper sloping edges inward, the upper folded edges swivelling down to lie along the vertical centre crease.

**4** Tease out the hidden corner from step 2.

**5** Allow the paper to flatten into the position shown. The hidden corner from step 2 will flatten to a point.

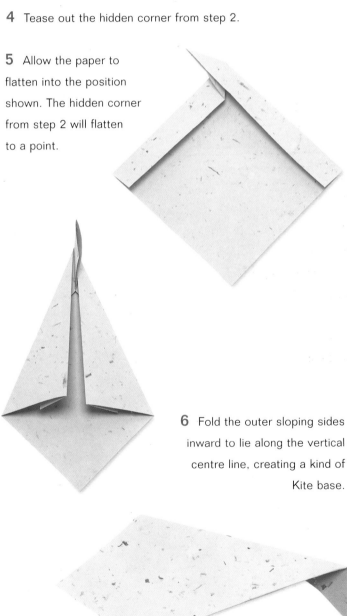

**6** Fold the outer sloping sides inward to lie along the vertical centre line, creating a kind of Kite base.

**7** Turn the model over.

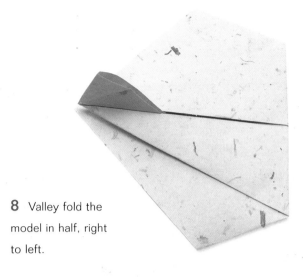

**8** Valley fold the model in half, right to left.

**9** Fold the model in half along the horizontal centre crease, bottom to top.

**10** Holding the outer layer of the model close to the lower edge with one hand, use your other hand to take hold of the inner point, and slide it upward away from you. Flatten the model with the inner point in its new position. The uppermost horizontal edge of the inner point should rest parallel to the lower horizontal edge of the outer section of the model. ▶

**11** Valley fold the upper corner of the outer section over, on a crease that runs along the edge of the inner point, at its resting place from step 10. Repeat on the reverse.

**12** To make the bowl, open out the small triangle at the end of the inner point, and pinch in a mountain-hinge fold at the base. This will keep the pocket open, ready to accept the projectile.

**13** To make the basketball hoop, fold a Waterbomb base at one end of the rectangle.

**14** Curl both of the sharp points inward, tucking one inside the other, until they stay in a hoop shape.

**15** Fold the outer vertical edges inward by 4–5cm/1½–2in. This amount is not critical.

**16** Open out the flaps folded in step 15 so that they rest at right angles to the centre portion of the model. Stand up the completed Basketball Hoop.

## HOW TO USE

Scrunch up a ball of paper, and place it in the bowl of the Catapult. Pull open the handles of the Catapult (the triangular flaps folded in step 11), so that the inner point swings forward.

The paper ball will be launched towards the hoop. See how many baskets you can score.

# moving lizard

This design is perhaps one of the cleverest action toys, skilfully created by Tomoko Fuse. The locking mechanism of the units, which allows the various sections of the body to swivel and move, is really quite amazing. You will need 12 sheets of paper, all the same size, and preferably green on one side; begin with this side face down in every case.

**1** To make the legs, fold and unfold the first square in half, then fold the outer horizontal edges to the centre crease.

**3** At the right-hand edge, fold the outer corners inward to meet the centre line.

**2** Turn the paper over.

**4** Unfold step 3.

**5** Fold the right-hand edge across to the left, on a vertical crease, which connects the ends of the diagonal creases made in step 3.

**6** The inner edge of the flap folded in step 5 is made from two layers of paper. Holding down the inner layer with one finger, pull the outer corner back to the right, squashing the paper to a point.

**7** Repeat step 6 with the lower half.

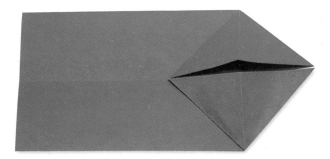

**8** Steps 6–7 completed.

**9** Fold the inner corner of this squashed diamond shape back out to the right, along the existing hinge crease.

**10** Valley fold the model in half along the long centre crease, bringing the top half down to rest on the lower section. The completed leg. Make three more legs in the same way.

**11** To make the head, begin at step 8 of the leg. Mountain fold the outer corners at the left underneath.

►

**12** To make the body, begin at step 8 of the leg, then repeat steps 3–8 at the left end of the model. Make three body sections.

**13** To make the tail, fold a kite base from another square, beginning with the green side face down.

**14** Narrow the model by folding the outer long edges to the centre line.

**15** Fold another square up to step 8 of the leg, then turn this unit over. Fold the corners at the left-hand edge inward to the centre crease. Make a really sharp crease.

**16** Unfold step 15, then insert the wider end of the tail section into the open-ended portion of this section.

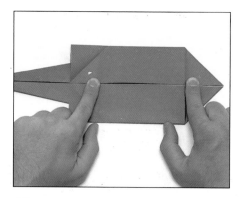

**17** Keep pushing the tail piece inward, until the tip reaches the vertical crease (where the right hand is indicating in the photograph).

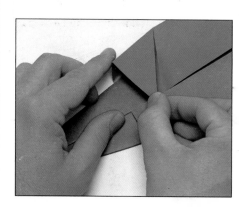

**18** Pinching the upper crease made in step 15 as a mountain fold, swivel the loose corner down, and, pulling the excess paper tightly over the tail piece, squash the paper flat into its new position.

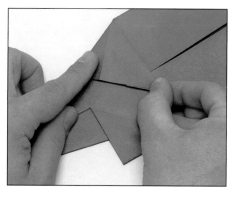

**19** Step 18 in progress.

**20** Step 18 completed. Note how there is now a tiny point projecting to the right of the vertical halfway line.

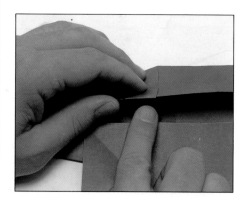

**21** Mountain fold the tip of this point inside, tucking it under the central raw edge.

**22** Repeat steps 18–21 on the other half of the model.

**23** Turn the tail section over.

**24** Take another sheet of paper, and, beginning with the green side face down, pre-crease in the vertical and horizontal halfway crease lines.

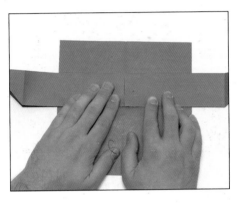

**25** Lay one pair of legs in the position shown, where the lower edges run along the horizontal centre crease of the flat sheet of paper, and where the two legs meet in the middle.

**26** Fold the upper corners down as far as they will comfortably go, the creases connecting the centre of the upper edge with the top edges of the legs.

**27** Fold the lower edge of paper upward on the existing halfway crease, wrapping the paper tightly over the two legs.

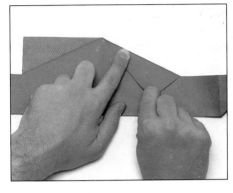

**28** Holding the assembly together, carefully turn the model over. Repeat step 26 on the upper corners.

**29** Make soft folds to the "thighs" of the lizard, by making diagonal creases, bringing lower edges to a vertical position, as shown. Turn the leg assembly over. Make another such assembly using the final sheet of paper, and the two other legs.

▶

**30** To join the head, body and tail section take the head section and one body section in either hand. Twisting one around slightly as you push them together, allow the slit in the end of one unit to slide between and into the slit in the end of the other, then twist to flatten out.

**31** Step 30 in progress.

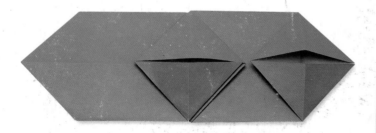

**32** Step 30 completed.

**33** Fold the opposite loose points of the central diamond section inward to lie along the vertical centre line, so that the two flaps lie together, as shown.

**34** Tuck the tips of these two flaps under the central horizontal raw edges, locking this side of the model.

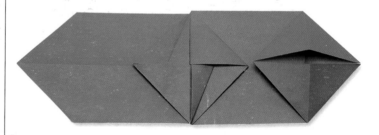

**35** Lock from step 34 completed.

**36** Turn the model over, and repeat steps 33–34 with the remaining points, to complete the lock on both sides.

**37** The two locked units can move freely.

**38** Assemble two more body units, and the tail section, as shown, in the same way as in steps 30–36.

**39** Slide the front leg assembly between the flaps of the two central diamond shapes of the body section nearest the head.

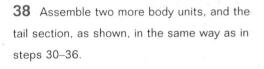

**40** Step 39 in progress.

**41** Finally slide the hind legs between similar flaps nearest the tail. The completed Moving Lizard.

# Practical
# Paper Folds

Making models that can actually be put to
use is extremely satisfying. You can make an elegant
and sturdy napkin ring, photoframe or business
card holder for everyday use or as an unusual gift.
Make sure that you choose your paper
carefully – the more hard-wearing it is the better.

# page corner

You will never lose your place in a book again
with this practical page corner designed by
Michael LaFosse. Michael is known for his
amazingly realistic animal designs, folded
from special paper that he makes himself, so it is
nice to see the other side of his work: simple models like
this one. A fairly small square, 7–8cm/2¾–3¼in, is an ideal size to use
for this model.

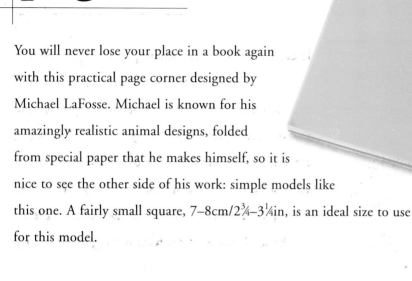

**1** Fold the paper in half diagonally. The
outer colour will be the colour of the
final model.

**2** Pinch-fold into quarters to mark the
halfway point of the lower edge, then
fold the single layer at the top down to
meet the lower edge.

**3** Fold the outer sharp points inward to
meet the pinch mark.

**4** Unfold the right-hand flap from step 3,
and now fold it to the uppermost corner.

**5** Using the crease made in step 3,
mountain fold the point and tuck it into
the pocket behind the horizontal folded
edge created in step 2.

**6** Repeat on the left side. The
completed Page Corner. The corner of
a page is slipped into the triangular
pouch, so that only the triangle shows
from the front.

# letterfold

There are many clever ways of producing letterfolds. These are methods of folding a letter into a self-locking form which can be sent through the post without the need for an envelope. This is one of the simplest, and a much-used favourite, thought to have been mailed anonymously many years ago, so that its origins are uncertain. A sheet of A4 (21 x 29cm/ 8¼ x 11½in) or any similar rectangle works fine.

**1** Begin by folding the shortest sides together, and unfolding, to determine the centre crease. Be sure that all the writing or print now faces you.

**2** Fold opposite corners at 45° to lie along the centre crease.

**3** Rotate the paper so that the original centre crease is now vertical to you. Fold the outer raw edges in to align with the inner raw edges.

**4** Rather like step 2, fold the now blunted corners at 45° to lie along the centre line.

**5** Tuck each of these loose flaps into the small triangular-shaped pockets beneath, to lock the model.

**6** Turn the model over. On the plain side, add the address of the person to whom you are sending the letterfold. Add a return-address label or other sticker to the reverse face, to secure the flaps, if you like.

# pin tray

Eric Kenneway is known for innovative folding sequences producing simple yet effective designs, as with this Pin Tray, which might also be used as a table decoration to hold party treats. Use a square of fairly stiff paper.

**1** Divide into thirds in both directions, to establish the crease pattern shown. If you pre-crease the diagonals first, the second direction that you fold into thirds is not the usual guesswork; simply line up the raw edge with those two points where the diagonals intersect with the first thirds creases.

**2** Begin with the colour side face down, and fold opposite outer edges to the first horizontal crease line, that is, one-sixth of the length of one side of the square.

**3** Rotate the paper 90° and fold the remaining two opposite sides inward, again by one-sixth, to meet up with the thirds creases.

**4** Hold the lower border with one hand, while taking hold of the partially hidden point with the other. Slide the point, and the excess paper, out to the side, then flatten. Repeat on the three remaining corners.

**5** Step 4 completed.

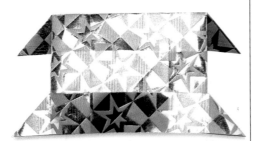

**6** Turn the paper over, then fold the outer edges to the horizontal centre line. The lower edge is shown already folded.

**7** Turn the model over once more.

**8** Holding on to the two points at the right-hand side with one hand, place your finger under the folded edge of the rectangular panel, and pull across, until the paper reaches the centre of the model. You should be able to squash fold the paper into a diamond shape. Repeat on the left-hand side.

**9** Step 8 completed at both ends.

**10** Valley fold the model in half, top to bottom.

**11** Lift up the model, and hold so that the longest sides are underneath. Place your fingers in the two pockets along the upper edges, and open the model out slightly, forming the two compartments of the Pin Tray. Allow the two sharp points at each end to lie one on top of the other.

**12** Tuck any one of these sharp points into the other; this is quite difficult to do.

**13** Finally, fold these interlocked points over as one completed section, resting each flap parallel to the base of the tray. Smooth out any creases with your fingers.

# the ellington

This is a napkin ring that was named after the street where the author was living at the time the idea for this book was conceived. The easiest way to prepare paper of an appropriate size is to trim off a 4cm (1½in) wide strip from the long edge of an A4 (21 x 29cm/8¼ x 11½in) sheet. The colour you begin with face down will be the only colour showing on the outside of the finished model.

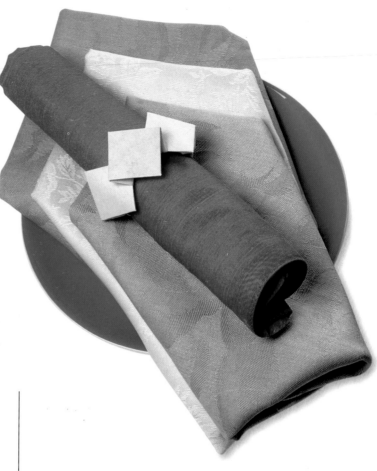

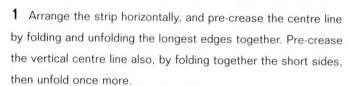

**1** Arrange the strip horizontally, and pre-crease the centre line by folding and unfolding the longest edges together. Pre-crease the vertical centre line also, by folding together the short sides, then unfold once more.

**2** Fold the lower edge at the right upward on a 45° crease so that it lies along the vertical centre line.

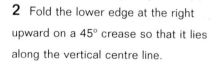

**3** Unfold step 2, then bring the upper right edge downward to lie along the vertical centre crease.

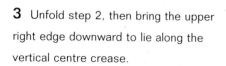

**4** Unfold step 3, then add a mountain crease vertically through the intersection of the two diagonal creases. In other words, you are pre-creasing a Waterbomb base. This is best achieved by folding the right-hand end of the paper behind, until the diagonal creases hitting the outer long edges meet. Crease through the paper, and unfold.

**5** Collapse the Waterbomb base on the creases formed in steps 2–4.

**6** Fold the upper portion of the strip back across to the right, as far as it will comfortably go (the crease will run along the edges of the inside-reverse-folded sections lying beneath).

**7** Fold the loose corners created in step 6 inward to lie along the horizontal centre line.

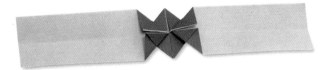

**8** Repeat steps 2–7 on the portion of the strip to the left of the vertical centre line.

**9** Fold the right-hand end of the strip upward to lie along the edge of the flaps folded in step 7.

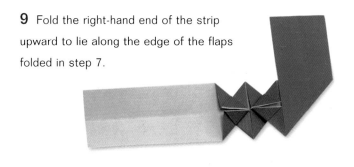

**10** Repeat steps 2–6 one more time at each end of the strip.

**11** Fold the upper and lower edges at each end of the strip inward to lie along the horizontal centre crease.

**12** Unfold step 11 once more. At one end of the paper, valley-fold over a very thin strip, while at the other end mountain-fold the edge over by a similar amount.

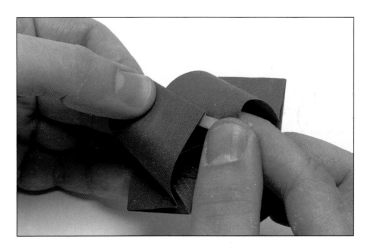

**13** Take hold of each end of the strip, and roll into a ring. When looking from the outside, you will hook the mountain-folded strip over the valley-folded strip from step 12.

**14** Lock the model together by carefully refolding the outer edges of the ring (pre-creased in step 11) inward to the centre line. Shape and curve the ring between fingers and thumbs.

# lazy susan

It is unusual to find a circular-shaped model in origami, yet this design has beautifully curved edges and is ideal as a table decoration, filled with nuts, sweets and other party treats. Use a fairly crisp, sturdy, square of paper, preferably duo (two-coloured).

**1** Begin by having the less dominant colour on top, and creasing in both diagonals. Then turn the paper over, and fold the paper in half in both directions, making the crease pattern shown. The main colour of the Lazy Susan will now be on top.

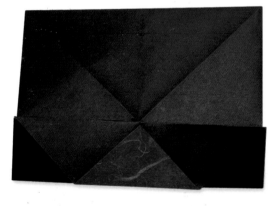

**3** Turn the paper over, and arrange as a square, so that you have horizontal and vertical sides. Fold the lower edge to the centre, creasing firmly across the model.

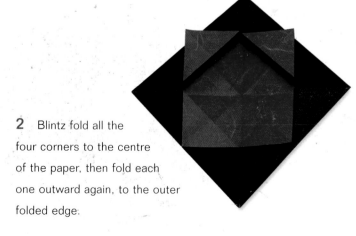

**2** Blintz fold all the four corners to the centre of the paper, then fold each one outward again, to the outer folded edge.

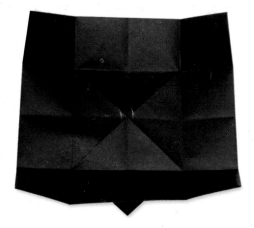

**4** Unfold step 3, and repeat with the three remaining edges, folding and unfolding each time.

**5** Turn the paper over. Outside the central square, use the diagonal creases and the creases made in steps 3–4, to pinch the paper backwards at the corners. You will notice that in the centre there is the crease pattern for forming a Waterbomb base.

**6** Push the centre inward, allowing it to sink inside, while collapsing the model.

**7** Flatten the model like a regular Waterbomb base.

**8** Using existing creases made in steps 3–4, inside reverse fold all the sharp points inside (front and back), allowing them to tuck in behind themselves. Flatten the model.

**9** Hold the model as shown. While carefully opening out one of the little pockets behind the upper edge, use your thumb to push up on the lower outside edge, curving it slightly.

**10** Repeat step 9 on the three remaining sides. Create the circular effect of the final model, and help to form the oval-shaped outer compartments.

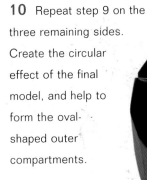
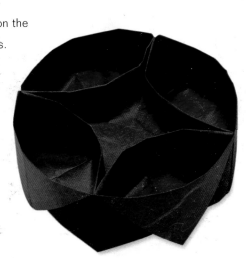

# photoframe

This model was designed by Larry Hart, who attempts, by his own admission, to create a 'masterpiece' at least once a decade; this is certainly his 1980s special. Use a sheet of A4 (21 × 29cm/8¼ × 11½in) paper, which will be the perfect size to house a 15 × 10cm/ 6 × 4in photograph. Fairly stiff parchment works extremely well. If you use paper with a pattern on one side, begin with that side face down; it will then appear on the corners of the final model.

**1** Fold the paper in half, bringing the shortest sides together.

**2** Fold into quarters, and unfold. The fold made in step 1 should be horizontal along the upper edge.

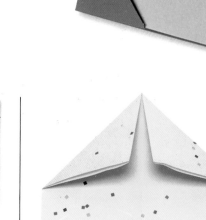

**3** Fold the two upper corners down to lie along the centre crease.

**4** Open out the flaps folded in step 3 and inside reverse fold them.

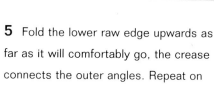

**5** Fold the lower raw edge upwards as far as it will comfortably go, the crease connects the outer angles. Repeat on the reverse side.

**6** Unfold step 5, then fold the top point down to meet the crease you have just made.

**7** Take hold of the top layer of paper, shaped like a tent, and, grasping the small triangular flap folded in step 6 as well, swing the outer flaps open.

**8** The paper will not lie completely flat, so you must now squash the excess paper at the centre, forming two triangles.

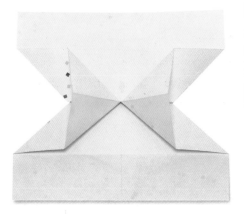

**9** Step 8 completed; the central area should resemble a bow tie.

**10** Fold the outer edges inward on existing creases, made in step 5.

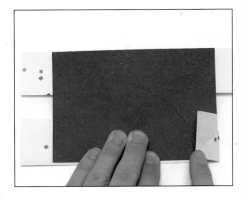

**11** Place the photograph, face up, horizontally lengthways on top of the model, and hold down in a central position with one hand. There are now four little flaps which project outwards beyond the corners. Fold these inward over the edge of the photograph.

**12** Step 11 completed.

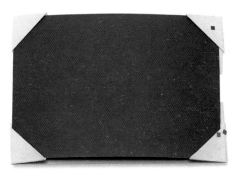

**13** Pull the photograph out from beneath these four flaps, then re-insert it into the four photo corners of the frame, as shown.

**14** There is a triangular flap on the reverse of the model; fold this out at an angle, so that the frame can be made to stand up. The completed Photoframe.

# square box

A variation on the traditional Masu Box, this model is folded in much the same way, except that when determining the position of the folds for the base, you need to divide the paper into thirds. You will need two sheets of fairly sturdy paper, the sheet for the lid will need to be slightly larger than the completed base of the box (see step 11). Begin with the colour required for the final box face down.

**1** Fold the paper in half corner to corner, and side to side in each direction, folding and unfolding each time, to determine the diagonal crease pattern.

**2** Blintz fold all four corners to the centre.

**3** Divide into thirds in both directions.

**4** Open out left and right blintzed corners completely.

**5** Using the existing thirds creases folded in step 3, raise the upper edge so that it projects upward at right angles to the base of the model. At the same time, raise the right-hand flap at right angles to the base, allowing the corner section to collapse as shown. There will be a small tuck formed in the paper, using existing creases.

**6** Step 5 completed.

**7** Repeat steps 5–6 with the lower edge, again forming the collapsing tuck in the paper.

**8** Fold the large excess flap formed by steps 5–7 inward over the outer edge of the box, to lock the model.

**9** Step 8 completed.

**10** Repeat steps 5–9 at the remaining open end of the model. The base of the box is completed.

**11** To make the lid, blintz fold a square of paper. The blintzed square should be larger than the opening of the box by approximately 2cm/¾in.

**12** Place the box in the centre of the paper, line it up squarely using the crease pattern and hold it firmly in place. Fold up one edge of the paper, so that it folds tightly to the side of the box. Pinch-fold a crease in the paper, to determine the base folds.

**13** Repeat step 12 carefully with the three remaining sides of the paper.

**14** Repeat steps 4–10, forming the lid of the box in the same way as the base of the box.

# business card holder

This is a variation on an original work by Professor Humiaki Huzita taught to the author by Susumu Nakajima. Practical wallet folds are common, and you might also use this design for stamps or credit cards. Leatherette paper with different colours on either side works superbly well. Begin with any sized rectangle; a sheet 22 x 26cm/8¾ x 10¼in was used here.

**1** Fold the paper in half, bringing the shorter sides together. The pockets for the cards will be of the colour now on the inside.

**2** Rotate the paper 180°, then fold the single lower edge up by a thin strip, about 1–2cm/½–¾in.

**3** Turn the paper over and repeat step 2 on the reverse side, matching up the folded edges.

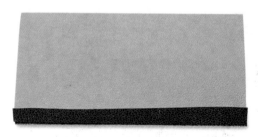

**4** Fold the lower edge (single layer only) upward, to a point approximately 3–4cm/1¼–1½in from the upper folded edge.

**5** Turn the paper over, and repeat on the other side. You can, if you wish, make the distances suggested in step 4 slightly different on each side.

**6** Open out step 4, and fold the lower corners on diagonal creases, to align with the horizontal centre crease.

**7** Refold step 4. Repeat on the reverse side.

**8** Open out the centre fold, as shown.

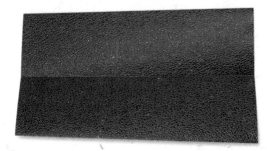

**9** Turn the paper over.

**10** At the left-hand side, fold the outer edge inward by approximately 1–2cm/½–¾in.

**11** Fold the right-hand edge over to the left, and tuck the corners into the two small triangular pockets.

**12** Step 11 completed.

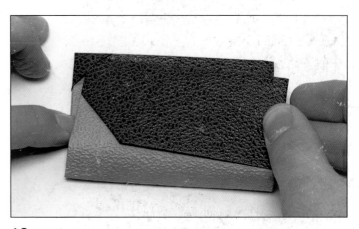

**13** Valley-fold the model in half along the original centre crease, and again tuck one side into the small triangular pocket on the other. This locks the model together.

# heart coaster

Francis Ow has designed hundreds of models on a heart theme, and this ingenious coaster is a favourite. Ideally use paper with a glossy surface such as sturdy paper-backed foil, so that it can be used practically as a coaster. You will need two squares of paper, preferably different colours; red and pink work very well. Begin with the final colour facing down.

**1** After folding and unfolding the first square in half, bottom to top, to determine the horizontal centre crease, fold upper and lower edges to the centre line.

**2** Turn the paper over, then at the left side, fold the two outer corners in to lie along the horizontal centre crease.

**3** Unfold step 2.

**4** Valley-fold the left-hand edge over to the right, making a vertical fold; this crease connects where the creases made in step 2 meet the upper and lower edges.

**5** Holding the upper portion of the flap folded in step 4 in place, slide the loose corner of the lower portion out towards you.

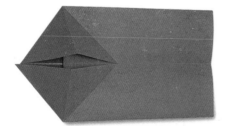

**6** Flatten the paper to a point. Repeat on the other side of the model.

**7** Repeat steps 2–6 at the other end of the paper.

**8** Turn the paper over. Fold the upper edge to the horizontal centre line, making a soft pinch-crease only through the central area of the paper, just to mark the halfway point between the centre and outer edge.

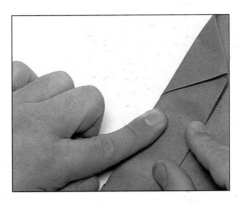

**9** Repeat step 8 on the lower edge. Unfold steps 8–9.

**10** Fold both outer edges inward to meet the pinch-creases made in steps 8–9.

**11** Steps 11–16 concentrate on one outer corner only. You will eventually need to repeat all these moves with the remaining three corners. Fold the lower right-hand sloping edge inward on a crease parallel to itself, as far as it will comfortably go, forming a narrow strip. This fold should connect with the angle at the bottom of the long side.

**12** Fold the upper corner of the paper, now overlapping the adjacent point, downward, so that the short upper edge comes to rest along the outer edge of the long strip folded in step 10.

▶

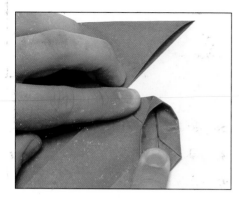

**13** Hold down the larger triangular section with one hand and use the other to fold the narrow strip back on itself so that it lies alongside the lower part of the strip. You will find that you need to make a small triangular squash fold which will form the cleft at the top of the heart.

**14** Step 13 in progress.

**15** Finally, tuck the loose point of the flap folded in step 13 under the long side border, to lock and neaten the corner of the model.

**16** Step 15 completed.

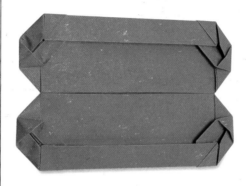

**17** Repeat steps 11–16 at the three remaining corners of the model. Turn the model over.

**BELOW** The completed Heart Coaster.

**18** Make another unit from the remaining square of paper. Looking at one unit, two hearts meet corner to corner at the centre of the paper. Lifting up any one corner of this unit, slide the main body of the second unit underneath.

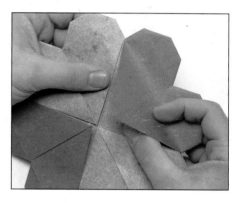

**19** Repeat at the opposite side of the first unit, lining up all four heart formations.

# easter basket

This model was designed by Aldo Putignano, and is one of a large collection of baskets, bowls and other containers created by this prolific folder. It is a classic to share around Easter time, and looks delightful filled with shredded yellow tissue and chocolate eggs. You will need a square of paper, preferably duo-coloured, and a strip of paper approximately the same length as a side of the square (see step 8).

**3** Fold the corner back up to the horizontal centre line.

**1** Begin with a Preliminary base; the outer colour will be the outer colour of the finished basket. The closed point should be towards you.

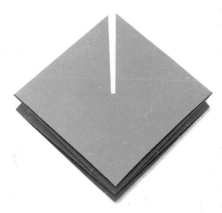

**2** Fold the single layer at the top down to the closed point at the bottom.

**4** Mountain fold the point inside, down as far as the crease made in the previous step. You might prefer to open out this triangular flap and use a valley crease, before refolding to the position shown.

**5** Double over the lower edge once more, producing a fairly thickly layered band around the middle of the model. Repeat steps 2–5 on the reverse face.

**6** There are two main flaps on either side of the vertical centre line. Fold the top flap at the right over to the left, using the vertical centre crease as a hinge crease and axis. Turn over and repeat on the reverse, again folding right over to left.

**7** Repeat steps 2–4 on the two new faces.

**8** Take a strip of paper, ideally the length of one side of the square you began folding the basket from. The width is up to you, but if you are using A4 (21 x 29cm/8¼ x 11½in) paper, you might consider using the portion cut off in making a square, sliced in half, short end to short end. Fold the two long edges to the centre. Then fold in half again, so that the handle is fairly stiff.

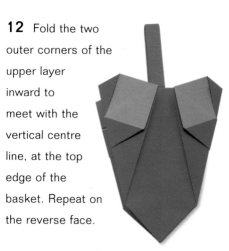

**9** Insert one end of the handle behind the flaps we formed as part of step 4. Push right down, until it can go no further.

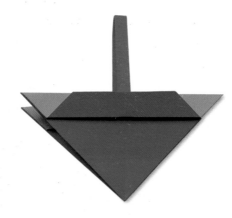

**10** Repeat step 5, doubling the section over, and locking the handle into place. Repeat steps 9–10 on the reverse face.

**11** Double over this entire section again, further locking the handle in place through the multiple creasing. Repeat on the reverse side.

**12** Fold the two outer corners of the upper layer inward to meet with the vertical centre line, at the top edge of the basket. Repeat on the reverse face.

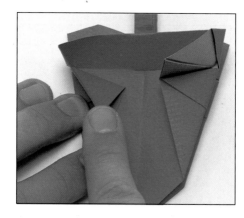

**13** As you look at the model you will see that there are two diamond shapes close to the top of the basket. Take hold of the top inner corner of this flap, and pull it towards you, making a crease that runs along the lower sloping edge. This will seem a fairly natural step. Repeat with the neighbouring flap.

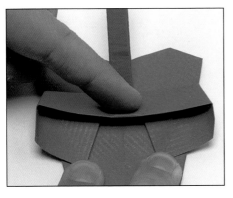

**14** Allow the horizontal folded edge behind the flaps to fold over to the front, squashing it flat on top of the two sections you have just folded. Repeat steps 13 and 14 on the reverse face.

**15** Steps 13 and 14 completed.

**16** There are now small flaps projecting outward from the natural shape of the basket. Mountain-fold all four behind and inside on themselves, using the edge of the basket as a guide (you might fold them over the basket's edge first, then refold, tucking them just behind the outer layer).

**17** Step 16 completed.

**18** This now leaves four small flaps pointing upward. Mountain fold these, and insert into a small triangular pocket that you will find behind them, formed by the diagonal folded edges of a previous step.

**19** To ensure the base is formed correctly, fold and unfold the lower point on a crease connecting the outer lower corners of the basket.

**20** Gently open out the basket by separating the two handle sections apart and hollowing out the final shape. Pinch creases where necessary to give a pleasing final form. Curve the handle and continue shaping the model.

**LEFT** The completed Easter Basket.

# pinwheel and puzzle purse

This variation on traditional themes first appeared in a small booklet of models published in 1972, written by British Origami Society member Eric Kenneway. There is a clever economy in the folding sequence, with the pre-creases all combining to produce a simple and delightful model. Use a square of fairly crisp paper, the colour intended for the outside of the purse face down.

**1** Begin by dividing the square into thirds in both directions. Also fold and unfold in half diagonally, adding further pre-creases.

**2** Turn the paper over. Fold the lower left corner upwards and across to the right, so that it meets with the lower left corner of the small square at top right.

**3** Unfold, then repeat step 2 with the remaining three corners, folding and unfolding each time.

**4** Turn the paper back over. Fold in the two adjacent outer edges, upper and right, as shown, using the existing thirds creases. This will bring the corner to a point.

**5** Squash the point down to the right.

**6** Using what is now a diagonal valley fold created in step 3, fold the inner horizontal edge of the uppermost flap outward, again bringing adjacent sides of the original square (this one and the next counter-clockwise) together in a point.

**7** Step 6 completed.

**8** Moving counter-clockwise, perform step 6 on the next side of the paper.

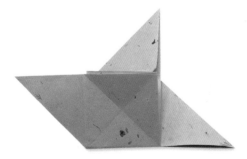

**9** Step 8 completed.

**10** Pull out the loose corner from behind the main flap folded in steps 8–9, swivelling the extra paper into a point once more.

**11** Step 10 completed.

**12** Fold the point created in step 10 downwards on the natural hinge crease. The completed Pinwheel. This can be attached to a stick, where it will spin in the wind.

**13** To transform into the Puzzle Purse, inside reverse fold the outer left corner through to the right, on a crease which runs along the edge of the central square.

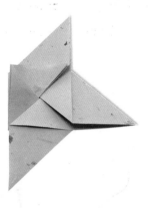

**14** Step 13 completed.

**15** Fold this loose point back on itself and tuck it into the pocket beneath (inside the diagonal folded edge of the triangular area found counter-clockwise).

▶

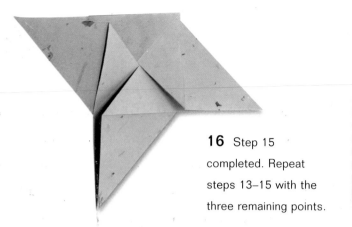

**16** Step 15 completed. Repeat steps 13–15 with the three remaining points.

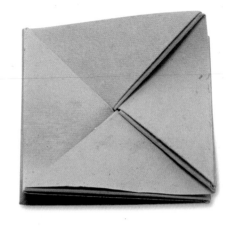

**RIGHT** The completed Puzzle Purse.

## HOW TO USE

**17** To open the Puzzle Purse, take hold of two opposite triangular areas at the sides between fingers and thumbs, single layer only.

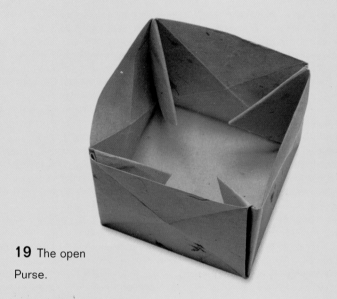

**19** The open Purse.

**18** Pull hands apart gently in opposing directions, allowing the model to twist open.

**20** To close, carefully twist the four corners according to the diagonal creases along the outside of the model, allowing the paper to collapse back flat.

# gift bag

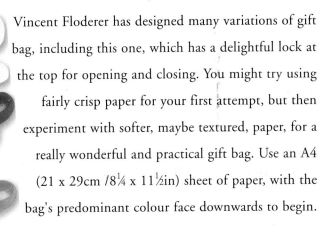

Vincent Floderer has designed many variations of gift bag, including this one, which has a delightful lock at the top for opening and closing. You might try using fairly crisp paper for your first attempt, but then experiment with softer, maybe textured, paper, for a really wonderful and practical gift bag. Use an A4 (21 x 29cm /8¼ x 11½in) sheet of paper, with the bag's predominant colour face downwards to begin.

**1** Begin by having the paper so that the longer sides are horizontal, then divide into thirds by folding and unfolding.

**2** Fold the lower left-hand corner in at 45° to lie along the horizontal crease line. Make a gentle crease, as this is only a guide for the main folds you will make later.

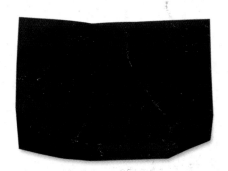

**3** Fold the right edge of the paper across to the left, so that it meets with the vertical edge of the small triangular flap folded in step 2.

**4** Unfold. Repeat steps 2–3 with the opposite sides of the paper.

**5** Unfold step 4, giving the crease pattern shown.

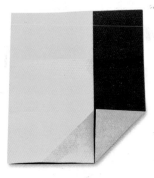

**6** Fold the lower edge at the left upward on a diagonal crease, so that it lies on the furthest vertical line, as shown. Pinch-crease only what will be a diagonal within the lower central square.

▶

**7** Unfold step 6.

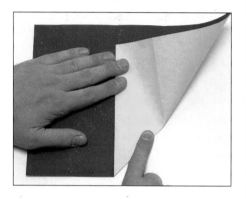

**8** Repeat step 6 using the lower right edge of the paper, again being careful to pinch-crease only within the lower central square.

**9** Step 8 completed.

**10** Repeat steps 6–9 at the top of the paper.

**11** Fold down the upper third, on the existing crease.

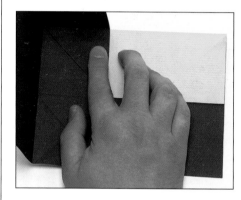

**12** Using the diagonal crease within the upper central square, valley-fold the raw edge outward. The model will now be three-dimensional.

**13** Repeat step 12 on the lower edge of paper, at the same end. The picture shows the model turned around, so that you can clearly see the box shape formed by steps 12–13. The second third of the paper overlaps the first.

**14** On the upper layer of the base, which is the small square visible inside the model, there is a small triangular flap, with a crease cutting across it. Using this crease, valley fold this triangular flap in half.

**15** Repeat with the portion of paper lying beneath this flap. By allowing the paper to form a three-dimensional box shape as in steps 12–14, you will find that the layers overlap,

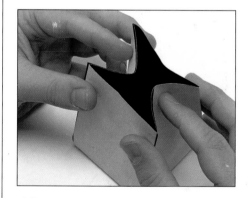

**16** Squeeze the front and reverse faces of the box shape together, allowing the two sides to collapse inward.

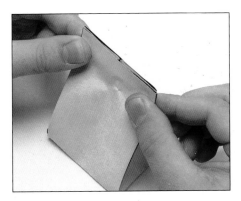

**17** Hold the collapsed paper together at the top.

**18** Fold the upper edge down, holding all layers together, by approximately 1cm/½in, or more if working with larger paper. This will make a border across the top of the model.

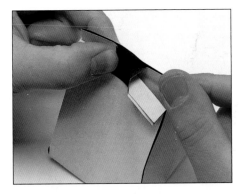

**19** Lift up and half unfold the outer layers of this horizontal border, allowing the central area within the layers to squash flat into the shape of a bow tie.

**20** Fold the section unfolded in step 19 over to the other side of the bag, to make the model symmetrical.

**21** To complete the lock, mountain-fold each of the upper corners behind, tucking them in-between the layers of paper at the sides.

**LEFT** The completed Gift Bag.

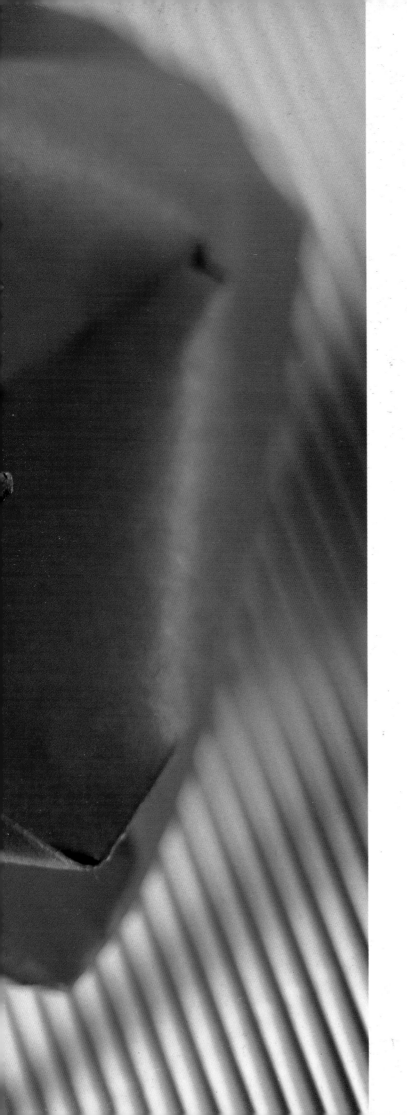

# Party Tricks

Origami is an extremely accommodating art, and there are many models that can be made from banknotes or newspaper, and others that illustrate a story or tell a fortune. All the models in this section are designed with an audience in mind, many of them are very simple, and with a little practice even the more complicated pieces can be made in minutes.

# laughter lines

This simple trick can be done with any banknote bearing a portrait, or, failing that, you can quite easily devise the same principle by drawing a "smiley" face on a sheet of paper, except leave the mouth a straight horizontal line. The creases will then go vertically through each eye, and be close to the corners of the mouth.

**1** Mountain fold the right hand edge of the note behind, making a sharp crease. If you are using a UK note this should go through one of the Queen's eyes.

**2** Unfold completely, and repeat step 1 using the Queen's other eye.

**3** Arrange the two existing creases at right angles, so that you appear to have the end of a box.

**4** Push the end (showing the centre of the Queen's face) inward, and squeeze the paper flat, allowing a valley fold to form between the two existing mountain folds.

**5** Open out the note, but do not pull flat; allow the V-shaped groove to remain in the paper. Now, if you look at the Queen's face straight on, she doesn't have much of an expression at all.

**6** Twist the note so that the upper edge moves away from you, while the lower edge moves closer. Now look, the Queen has a smile.

**7** If you now twist the note the other way, so that the upper edge moves closer while the lower edge moves further away, you will see a very miserable monarch indeed. The completed Laughter Lines.

# fortune teller

This has to be the one model that virtually everyone remembers making as a child at school. It works like this: write four different colours on the outer petals of the completed model, number the eight panels on the inside, and underneath each panel write a "fortune". Ask a friend to name a colour, and then open and close the teller according to the number of letters that spell the chosen colour. The friend then chooses one of the visible numbers, and the teller is then opened and closed this number of times. The process is repeated, and, finally, the innermost flap is lifted to reveal the fortune.

**1** Blintz fold the corners of a square. Turn the paper over and Blintz fold again.

**2** Fold the model in half, bottom to top, then hold it as shown, and collapse Preliminary-base-style, using existing creases.

**3** Step 2 completed.

**4** Pull open the raw blintzed flaps folded in step 1.

**5** Place fingers and thumbs into the four respective pockets created in step 4. The Fortune Teller can be flexed by first separating your two fingers from your two thumbs, and then separating your two hands, while pinching with each.

**6** The secondary blintzed flaps folded at the end of step 1 are lifted up to reveal the fortune.

# dollar shirt

This is an impressive traditional fold that is always popular at parties. You can ask to "borrow" a banknote from one of your audience and promise to show the owner a Gambler's Fold. At the conclusion, you can assure him that he need not worry about losing his money as he can "bet his shirt that he will get his money back". This can also be made using duo paper, as used here.

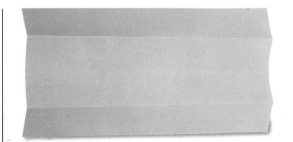

**1** The illustration shows the model folded from a 2:1 (half a square) sheet of paper. The colour you begin with on top will form the collar and cuffs. If folding from most currencies of bank note, you will be able to make a fairly well-proportioned model from the note as it is. If folding from a US dollar, it is wise to make an extra fold to begin with, to change the proportions of the note: on the portrait face, fold one short side inward, to meet with the outside edge of the circular "frame". Then treat the note in the same way as any other. After folding and unfolding the paper in half, bringing the two longest sides together, fold these edges inward to the centre crease, then arrange the paper as shown.

**2** Unfold step 1 and turn the paper over.

**3** At the right, fold a thin strip, about 5mm–1cm (¼–½in) in width, revealing the colour for the collar.

**4** Turn the paper over, and refold the long sides into the centre.

**5** At the right-hand end, fold the reverse coloured strip behind, on a crease that runs along the edge, so that you are doubling the paper over by the same amount again.

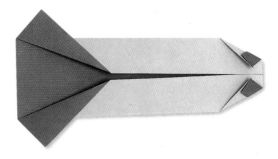

**6** Fold the right-hand corners inward to meet the horizontal centre line. The corners rest at a point a short distance in from the right-hand edge, making creases which meet the outer edges at a fairly obtuse angle, as shown. This forms the collar. At the left-hand end of the model, fold the inner flaps outward, as far as they will comfortably go, that is to the extreme lower and upper corners. The angle of the fold is not critical, but you should have a small triangle projecting above and below the model. These folds will form the sleeves.

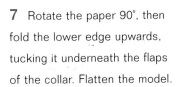

**7** Rotate the paper 90°, then fold the lower edge upwards, tucking it underneath the flaps of the collar. Flatten the model.

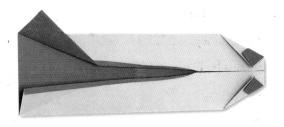

**8** If you wish to add cuffs to the sleeves, unfold the model back to step 6, then also unfold the flaps that make the sleeves. Fold the long inner edges evenly outward, folding a very thin strip, from the open edge up to or slightly beyond the centre of the model. Do not worry if these two folds do not run level or meet, as this section of the paper will be hidden away on the final model. Then refold the sleeve flaps outward on existing creases. The photograph shows the lower flap with the necessary fold for the cuff. The upper flap shows the sleeve fold completed.

**9** Finally, refold step 7 to complete the dollar shirt with cuffs.

# envelope trick

Ed Sullivan designed a very clever model called an Un-unfoldable Box, which, as the name implies, was, once folded, impossible to unfold without tearing the paper. The principle used in this model lends itself to this trick with an ordinary envelope. Use a fairly stiff manilla office envelope, say A4 (21 x 29cm/8¼ x 11½in) in size.

**1** For this trick, you trim the sealing flap from an envelope, and cut the top down by 1–2cm/½–1in, leaving raw edges. Then, using the following folding technique, secretly fold the raw edges completely outside on themselves. The idea of the trick is to show your friend the envelope so that he or she can see the folded edge, then you cut off the fold, leaving raw edges once again, and invite your friend to fold it again. Of course he or she will not be able to do so without tearing the paper and getting into a mess.

**2** You now demonstrate how the trick is done. Fold the open end (both edges folded as one) over by 2–3cm/¾–1¼in.

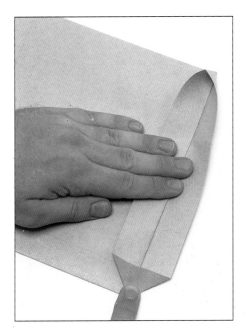

**3** Unfold just the single upper layer folded in step 2, causing you to make two small triangular squash folds at each outer corner of the envelope.

**4** Turn the envelope over.

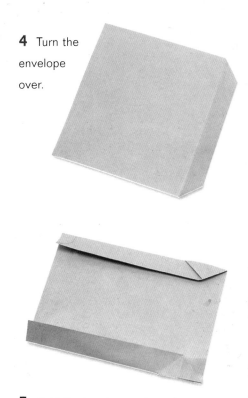

**5** Fold the two long outer edges inward, along the edges of the squash folds made in step 3.

**6** Turn the model over, and mountain-fold the remaining outer edge of the envelope behind, as far as it will comfortably go. Now, each edge at the opening has been folded down, one either side.

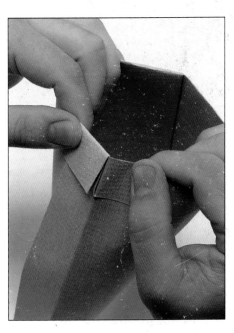

**7** Carefully place your fingers inside the opening of the envelope, and hold one corner between fingers and thumbs.

**8** With extreme care, pull your hands apart, allowing the paper at the corner to stretch, and the excess hidden paper to be pulled free. Pull very slowly, until all the trapped paper is released.

**9** Step 8 completed. Repeat at the other corner of the envelope. You will now have the same result as illustrated earlier: the end of the envelope will have been completely turned outside on itself.

# blinking eyes

This cheeky action model was created by Jeremy Shafer. There are many variations on the same theme, with the same mechanism creating a mouth as well, and including four neighbouring heads out of one sheet of paper, making a barbershop quartet. The predominant colour for the final model should begin face down. Use a square of fairly thin, crisp paper.

**1** Pre-crease the halfway horizontal centre line, and the vertical halfway centre line. Fold and unfold each time.

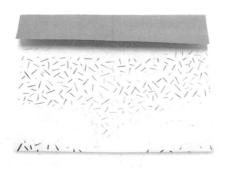

**2** Fold the upper edge down to meet the horizontal crease.

**3** Fold the lower edge about 3mm/⅛in higher than the halfway crease, then allow this flap to tuck underneath the first.

**4** Turn the paper over. Fold in a thin strip of paper, about 3mm/⅛in, at each of the shortest sides.

**5** Double over once more the strips folded in step 4.

**6** Turn the model over and fold the outer edges to the centre.

**7** Collapse the model, mountain folding along the vertical centre crease.

**8** Turn the model over. Opening out one half of the model slightly, reach inside and pull the upper raw edge out towards you, causing an inside reverse fold to be incorporated into this section, as you refold the paper flat. Allow the paper to be pulled out as far as it can go.

**9** Step 8 in progress: shaping the upper eyelid.

**10** Repeat with the other half.

**11** Repeat steps 8–10 with the remaining raw edges, forming the lower eyelids.

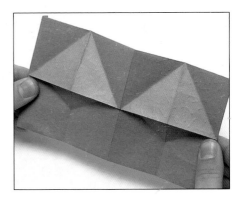

**12** Hold the model at either end. If you allow the paper to collapse naturally, the eyes will appear open.

**13** If you pull the ends fairly taut, the eyes will appear closed. Move your hands inward, then outward, to create the Blinking Eyes.

# strawberry

This design by Rae Cooker makes an admirable alternative to the well-known traditional waterbomb. It is fun to fold as a party trick because there is a surprise finale as you inflate the model. If you are fortunate enough to find some giftwrap with red on one side and green on the reverse, this will be ideal.

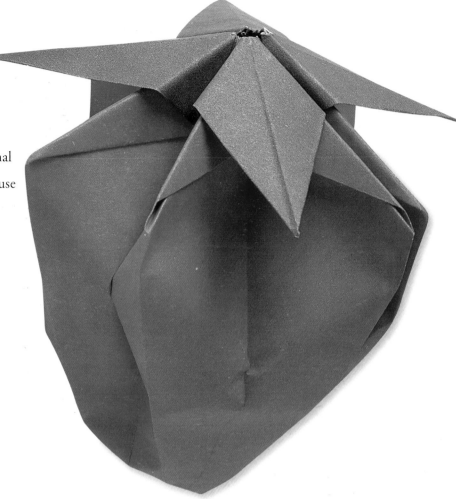

**1** Beginning from a red-coloured Preliminary base, squash all the four large flaps into the final step of the Frog base.

**2** Using the vertical hinge crease as an axis, fold one of the large flaps at the right across to the left, to reveal a plain-coloured face.

**3** Fold each of the lower sloping edges, single layer only, inward to lie along the vertical centre crease.

**7** Fold each of the lower short edges upward to lie along the vertical centre line. The crease extends to the outermost corners left and right.

**4** Fold the lower corner, single layer only, upward as far as it will comfortably go.

**8** Repeat step 7 on the three remaining similar faces.

**10** Carefully use your fingers and thumbs to flip up all four of these reverse-coloured flaps (the stalk), so that they form a "propeller" at the top of the model.

**5** Repeat steps 3–4 on the remaining three plain faces. You will need to repeat step 2 on the reverse face, then rotate the layers in turn to make this possible.

**6** Step 5 completed: Rotate the layers once more so that you have a plain face on top.

**9** There are eight large flaps in total, around the central axis. Separate them into pairs, causing the model to appear three-dimensional, and hold between fingers and thumbs in-between each pair of flaps. The grouping should be such that your fingers and thumbs lie upon the green points folded in steps 4–5.

**11** Now take a deep breath, place your lips right up to the hole at the top of the model, and give a good sharp blow into the strawberry. It will magically inflate. If you blow too hard, you will end up with a tomato!

# kissing lips

Designed by Soon Young Lee, this has to be one of my all-time favourite action models. You begin by making a series of folds, only to unfold everything back to the original square. You then refold all the existing creases in a new sequence to produce a final model of elegant simplicity yet delightfully comic working. Use a square of crisp paper, preferably red on one side. Begin with this side uppermost.

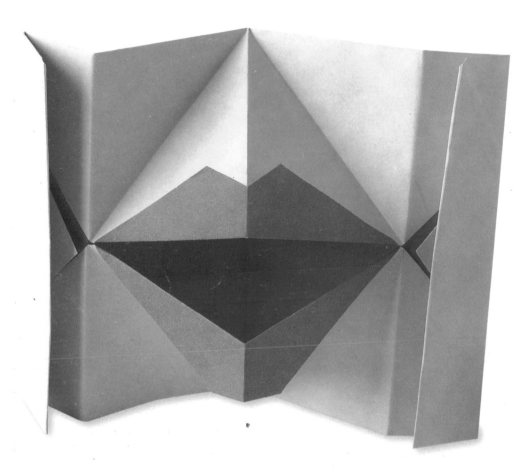

**1** Fold the paper in half diagonally.

**2** Fold the sharp point at the right over to the left, a third of the entire distance of the horizontal edge.

**3** Fold the sharp point at the left over to the right in the same way.

**4** Fold each point in turn to meet with the upper corners, as shown.

**5** Now fold each point down to the lower corners, as shown.

**6** Swivel the sloping edge of the small triangular flaps to lie along the folded edges made in step 5.

**7** There will now be two tiny triangular points projecting out from the sides of the model. Fold these in half, folding the tips downward, as shown.

**8** Open out every fold made thus far, and arrange so that the reverse colour is now uppermost, and all the creases are at the upper and lower corners of the paper.

**9** Using the creases made in step 7, fold in the tips of each opposite corner.

**10** Using the creases made in step 6, fold the two upper edges inward to form rabbit ears with each opposite corner.

**11** Turn the paper over, and use existing creases formed in steps 2–3 to fold each opposite corner section in to the middle. The paper should not be forced to flatten here, but allowed to be left slightly three-dimensional, so that the two lips are not damaged.

**12** Fold the whole model in half side to side, allowing the V shape of creases folded in step 4 to re-form. One of the creases in this V is currently a mountain, where both should be valley folds. Manually change the mountain to a valley on both lip sections, before making this collapse. ▶

**13** Step 12 completed.

**14** Fold the single upper layer away from you as far as it will comfortably go. The corners meet logically.

**15** To hide the colour of the large diamond shape, fold the raw corner back towards you, as shown.

**16** Double the folded edge created in step 15 over once more, creating a rectangular section. This is the area of paper held when working the model.

**RIGHT** The completed kissing lips.

## HOW TO USE

Repeat steps 14–16 on the reverse face. Hold the model between fingers and thumbs, by the two side panels made in step 16. This double-folded section needs to be raised to rest at 90° to the rest of the model.

Pull gently apart, so that the lips "kiss". With a little ingenuity, you can mount the lips inside the folded spine of a card, to produce a pop-up kiss card.

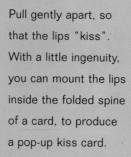

# money pig

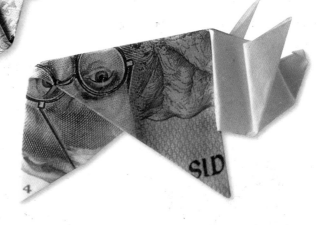

This design by Paul Jackson has been slightly simplified so that it can be made quickly. If the banknote isn't quite 2:1 in proportion (British £5 notes are the closest to it), then perhaps use a very fine fold or two down either edge to match this proportion. Here, the model is seen made from paper. Preferably use paper that is the same colour on both sides, as both sides of the paper show on the final model.

**1** Pre-crease the vertical centre line by folding and unfolding the shortest sides together. Turn the paper over, so that the crease you have made appears now as a mountain fold. Arrange the paper so that the longest edges are horizontal.

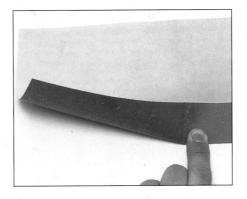

**2** Valley-fold the horizontal centre crease by folding and unfolding bottom to top. Then fold the lower long side to the horizontal centre crease, but only crease from the vertical centre line outward to the right side.

**3** Unfold step 2, and repeat with the upper edge. Unfold the paper completely.

▶

**4** Fold the right edge across to the left, so that it lies along the vertical centre line. Unfold once more.

**5** The paper is turned around here for clarity. Take hold of the vertical centre crease (the mountain fold) between fingers and thumbs, as shown. Slide the paper away from you, until you can bring the mountain-folded edge down to lie along the crease made in step 4. Flatten the model.

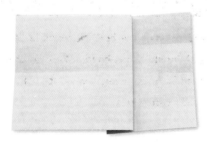

**6** Step 5 completed.

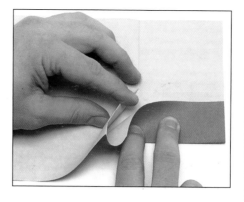

**7** At the right-hand side, refold the outer edges into the horizontal centre line made in step 2. Beneath the pleat formed in steps 5–6, you will need to make a 45° diagonal fold across the underside of the pleated section.

**8** Step 7 completed.

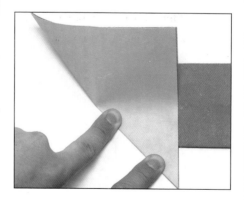

**9** Turn the paper over, but keep it arranged in the same way. Fold the square at the left in half diagonally, bringing the lower edge to lie along the vertical edge. Crease only between the lower right corner of this square and the centre. Unfold.

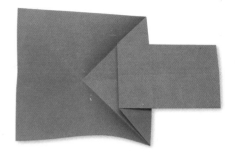

**10** Repeat step 9 folding the upper edge to the vertical edge, creasing in the same way, and unfolding.

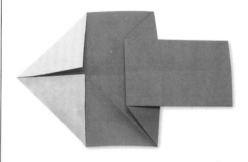

**11** Fold the two left corners inward to lie along the horizontal centre crease.

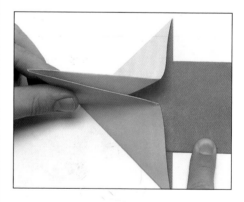

**12** Using the two creases made in steps 9–10, and the left-hand half of the horizontal centre crease, pinch the left corner to a point, forming a kind of rabbit ear.

**13** Allowing the rabbit ear fold in step 12 to open out slightly, lift the section of paper from beneath (the pleated portion), and let it rest on top of the raised point.

**14** Valley fold the model in half along the horizontal centre crease, and, as you do so, push the section of paper released in step 13 in-between the layers of the raised point. This will lock the model together well, and help prevent the legs splaying apart.

**15** Suggest the pig's tail by making a valley/mountain pleat in the upper left corner. At the right, fold the short vertical edge upward, single layer only, to lie along the upper edge.

**16** Unfold the lower right corner, then inside reverse fold it.

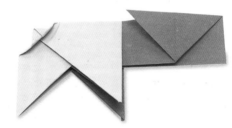

**17** Swing the point created by step 16 across to the left.

**18** Fold the sloping edge of this point upward to a vertical position. This is the ear.

**19** Repeat steps 15–18 on the reverse face of the head. Make two inside reverse folds at the front of the head, first of all reversing the point inside the head, then with another reverse fold closer to the point, reverse the paper back out again, to suggest the snout. Turn the tip of the snout outside on itself; you will need to open the point up slightly from below to be able to do this.

**20** Holding the body between finger and thumb of one hand, take hold of the head with the other, and crimp fold the head down slightly.

**LEFT** The completed Money Pig.

# newspaper hats

It is not often that one model can be turned into several others during the folding sequence, but that is what happens here. In this fun party piece, simple paper hats are transformed in sequence, beginning with a Party Hat, which becomes a Printer's Hat, then a Jester's Hat, a Teacher's Mortarboard and, finally, a Bishop's Mitre. Begin this traditional idea with a large double-spread newspaper. There are probably lots of other hats that might be added to the sequence, using a little of your imagination.

**1** Begin by folding the sheet of newspaper in half, bringing the shorter edges together. Then fold in half again (into quarters) and unfold, to establish the vertical centre crease. Making sure that the folded edge now lies along the top, bring both upper corners down to lie along the vertical centre line.

**3** Double this thin strip over once more.

**2** Fold the lower edge upward, single layer only, to lie along the lower edge of the triangular flaps folded in step 1.

**4** Turn the model over.

**5** Fold the two outer edges into the vertical centre line.

**6** Fold the lower edge up to lie along the lower edge of the narrow border established in step 3.

**7** Unfold step 6. Fold the lower outer corners inward to lie along the horizontal crease made in step 6.

**8** Fold the lower portion upward as far as it will comfortably go, i.e. over the edge of the narrow border created in step 3.

**9** Using the horizontal crease made in step 6, mountain fold the end strip of this flap into the pocket behind the narrow border created in step 3. Flatten the model.

**10** Step 9 completed.

**11** Fold the upper corner down to the lower edge, tucking it under the border created in step 9.

**12** Open out the lower edges, hollowing the paper out slightly, while pushing the upper crease inward, to soften and curve.

**13** This forms the Party Hat.

▶

**14** Turn the model over. Pull the front and rear sides of the hat in opposite directions.

**15** Then squash the paper flat into a diamond shape.

**16** With the narrow border horizontal top and bottom, fold the lower corner up to the centre, and tuck it underneath this border.

**17** Repeat step 16 with the upper corner.

**18** Open out the central slit, with fingers or thumbs under the narrow borders, pulling in opposite directions.

**19** Use fingers and thumbs to pinch-crease around the already established fold lines, thus forming a box shape.

**20** Turn the model over. The completed Printer's Hat.

**21** Pull out the two triangular flaps from beneath the narrow border (folded in steps 16–17) and allow them to rest, pointing at a slightly downward slope. The completed Jester's Hat.

**22** Pull out the triangular flap folded in step 11, and arrange all three points so that they are parallel to your folding surface. The completed Teacher's Mortarboard.

**23** Take hold of the point released in step 22, and lift it up, allowing the paper to open up a little more.

**ABOVE** The completed Bishop's Mitre.

# the captain's shirt story

After folding the traditional paper boat, ideally from a spread of newspaper, you can tell your audience the story of the Captain's Shirt, where, by tearing the paper, you can produce a surprising result. Such paper tricks are quite common, and sometimes a pre-printed sheet is folded in a certain way so that it will provide the punchline to the joke.

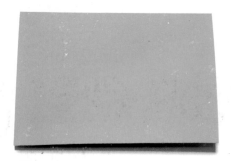

**1** To make the boat, fold the paper in half, bringing the two shorter sides together. Rotate the paper 180°, so that the fold you have just made now runs along the upper edge.

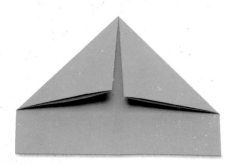

**2** Fold the paper in half again, side to side, to establish the vertical centre crease. Unfold, then fold both of the upper corners down to lie along the crease just made.

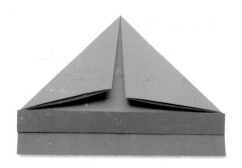

**3** Fold the lower edge (single layer only) up to lie along the edges of the flaps folded in step 2.

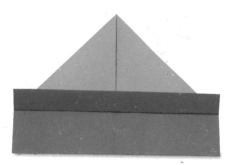

**4** Fold the lower edge over once more, doubling the thickness of the horizontal band.

**5** Repeat steps 3–4 on the reverse face, then open out from below what is the traditional paper hat. Push the two end corners of the hat together, until eventually the model can be flattened into a diamond shape. At the opening the ends of the borders folded in steps 3–4 will need to be overlapped.

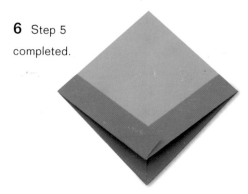

**6** Step 5 completed.

**7** Fold the lower corner up (single layer only) to a point approximately a third of the way up the height of the hat. Repeat on the reverse face.

**8** Separate the front and rear sides of the model, while pushing the outer edges together. You are simply repeating step 5 only in reverse. Flatten the model.

**9** Fold the lower edge (single layer only) upward as far as it will comfortably go. Repeat on the reverse face.

**10** Hold the boat firmly in one hand, while using the other to tease out the point carefully that lies behind the wide band folded in step 9. Keep pulling the point out until you can flatten the model once more. Repeat at the other end.

**ABOVE** The boat completed.

## HOW TO USE

You can tell the story as elaborately as you like. Essentially it goes like this:

*"There was once a sea captain, who, not being very clever, decided to set sail in a boat made of paper. No sooner had the first signs of a storm come up than he began to get very worried. His fears proved justified when lightning struck the prow of the boat and tore it off. "*

At this point, you hold the boat tightly in one hand and tear off one end. Tear in a circular motion from halfway along the upper deck, around to the lower corner of the boat.

*"Yet more lighting struck the boat, and the distraught captain watched as the stern was destroyed …"*

Tear off the other end of the boat in the same way

*"…Then with a loud crash the mast and sails were torn down by the wind."*

Tear off the remaining point in a circular motion beginning halfway along the edge of each sail.

At the end of the story, you open out the paper as shown, and say:

*"And there was nothing left but the Captain's Shirt!"*

# Decorative Origami

Whether you want to make everyday origami

decorations such as napkin folds, or prefer to save

your origami skills for special occasions, such as

Christmas, Valentine's Day, birthdays and other

anniversaries, this section is packed with attractive

decorative origami ideas for individual gifts and to

decorate the table and the home.

# sailboat

This traditional design is also the logo for the American origami society, called OUSA (Origami USA). It is a wonderful model for teaching, and makes a fine place setting at children's parties with the name of each party guest written on the hull. Ideally use duo paper.

**1** Begin with the Preliminary base, the outer colour will be the colour of the hull, the inner colour the sails. Begin with the open flaps at the top.

**2** Mountain fold the outer single layer at the top behind and down inside the model. Repeat on the reverse side, then flatten.

**3** Make two valley folds to one of the sails, the first pulling the point down over the hull, the second, folding it back up again, making a narrow pleat in the paper. This brings the sail back to a position a little lower than the other, giving a small sail and a large sail.

**4** Pull the upper edge of the hull out a little, and allow the pleat to tuck in behind it, out of sight.

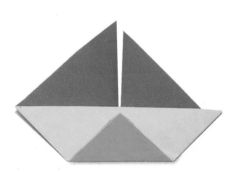

**5** Fold the lower point up to meet with the upper edge of the hull.

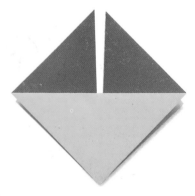

**6** Partially unfold step 5, bringing the triangular flap to rest at right angles to the boat. This will allow the sailboat to free-stand.

# hanging decoration

Tomoko Fuse is famous for designing all kinds of elaborate modular constructions and beautiful boxes with unusual patterned lids. Occasionally, however, she has introduced simple, practical models like this decoration, one end of which can be threaded up for hanging. You will need two identically sized sheets of crisp paper, preferably with reverse colours.

**1** Begin with a Preliminary base, with the closed point at the top. The outer colour will be the predominant colour of the final model.

**2** Upper layer only, fold the two sloping sides in to meet the vertical centre line.

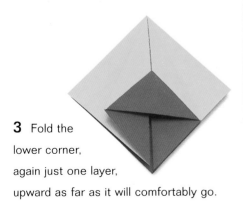

**3** Fold the lower corner, again just one layer, upward as far as it will comfortably go.

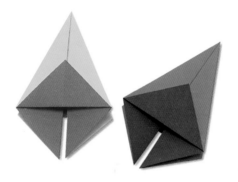

**4** Repeat steps 2 and 3 on the reverse face. Make a second unit in exactly the same way.

**5** Make the units three-dimensional by separating the main flaps. There are spaces in between each of the flaps on each unit. In one space, you will notice the small triangular flap folded in step 3. The adjacent space is plain. Rotate the main flap on each unit, so that in each case two sections show triangular flaps, while the others show plain faces.

**6** Now insert one unit into the other, making sure that all the way around the model the plain point goes underneath the triangular flap created in step 3. This will happen four times, in alternate directions.

**7** Once all the points are correctly inserted into the respective pockets, continue pushing the two units together to completely lock the two halves.

# bangle

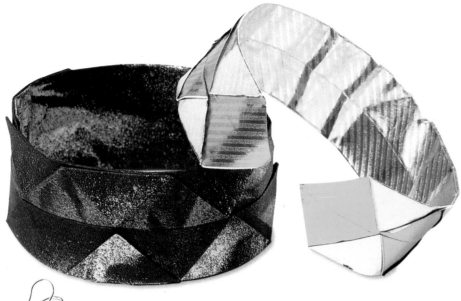

This is a fairly traditional method of pleating opposite diagonal corners of a square back and forth to create a diamond-triangle, reverse-colour pattern. Follow the steps carefully, as this is a very logical model in terms of where each of the horizontal creases are located: first, the paper is divided into eighths, then into sixteenths on the reverse side of the paper.

Brightly coloured metallic foil with a different reverse colour works very well. It doesn't really matter which side you begin with face up, as there is a fairly even colour distribution in the final pattern of the bangle.

**1** Always keeping the paper arranged as a diamond, that is with one corner pointing towards you, fold and unfold the paper in half, corner to corner in both directions, to determine the diagonal creases.

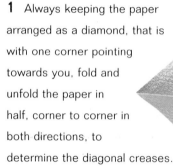

**2** Blintz fold the upper and lower corners to the centre.

**3** Unfold the lower corner, then fold it back inwards to meet the intersection of the vertical diagonal and the horizontal crease line folded in step 2.

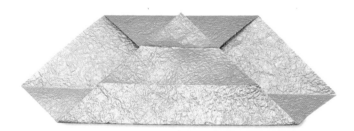

**4** Unfold the lower corner once more, and then fold it to meet the centre of the upper folded edge.

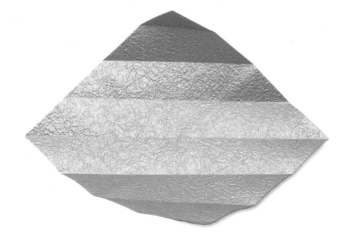

**5** Unfold completely. Now, if you restore the Blintz fold from step 2 with the lower corner, you can repeat steps 3–4 with the upper corner, making similar horizontal creases. When you open out the paper completely, you will have divided it into eight equal horizontal bands.

**6** Turn the paper over. Keep the paper arranged so that all the creases, now appearing as mountain folds, are horizontal. Fold the lower corner up to meet with the intersection of the vertical diagonal and the nearest crease.

**7** Unfold step 6. Then, counting upward two more intersections (to one eighth-crease short of the horizontal diagonal) fold the lower corner once more, to make another sixteenth-division crease.

**8** Unfold step 7. Then fold the lower corner to the intersection of the vertical diagonal and the eighth-crease beyond the horizontal diagonal (again skipping one eighth-crease to the next). Make another sixteenth pre-crease.

**9** Finally, fold the lower corner to meet the intersection of the vertical diagonal and the very last eighth-crease.

**10** Unfold the paper, and repeat steps 6–9 with the upper corner. It is easier to do this by rotating the paper 180° so that you are folding away from you. The completed crease pattern.

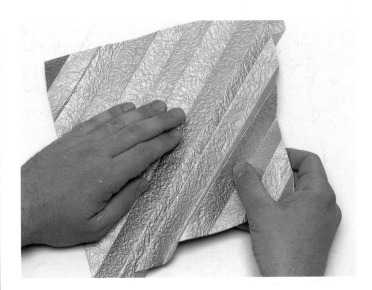

**11** Rotate the paper around so that all the creases made in steps 2–10 are running diagonally to you. Carefully begin to collapse all the existing valley and mountain folds of one half of the model, pleating back and forth as shown.

▶

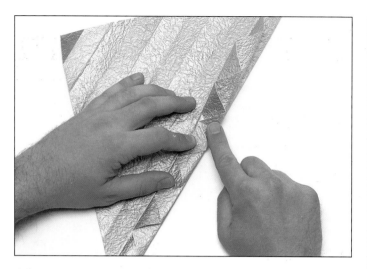

**12** Step 11 completed on the right side of the model.

**13** Repeat step 11 on the left side of the model.

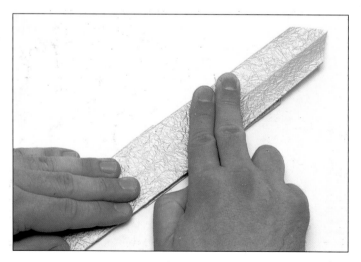

**14** Turn the paper over, and run your fingers over the model to really press the pleats flat. It is easier to do this on the reverse side of the paper so that you do not tear the raw edges of the patterned areas.

**15** Take hold of either end of the strip, and roll the paper into a ring, tucking one end into the pocket created by the pleated sections of the other end. Slide the end in beneath these pleats, and push in until you have a complete, regular pattern of diamonds and triangles.

**16** Shape and curve the bangle, which will also give tension to the overlapped area, thus helping the lock stay together.

# bishop's mitre napkin

Here is the folding method for a very popular napkin fold. Ideally, use a square, starched material napkin. As a variation on the mitre, you can peel down the two outer points to form a fleur-de-lys.

**3** Fold this corner back down to the lower horizontal edge.

**4** Carefully turn the napkin over.

**1** Begin by folding the napkin in half diagonally, then fold the sharp corner at the left up to the top.

**2** Fold the right corner up to the top, then fold the lower corner up to a point a short distance down from the top, leaving a border along the adjacent upper edges.

**5** Carefully roll the napkin into a cylinder, bringing the left and right sides together, and tuck one side into the diagonal folded edge of the other created in step 2. In the photograph, the right side is being tucked into the left side pocket. Stand upright.

# pixie boot napkin

For this traditional design you might use either a material napkin, as shown, or a paper napkin. If using the latter, be sure to fold it carefully, to avoid tearing the paper. It isn't always easy to find perfectly square napkins, so you may need to "improvise" a little with the folding method. The ideal place to display this model is in the centre of a plate.

**1** Fold the napkin in half, lower edge to upper edge.

**2** Fold in half again, lower edge to upper edge.

**3** Pre-crease the short vertical centre line, then fold the lower edges upward on diagonal creases, to lie along this centre line.

**4** Fold the outer sloping sides into the centre line.

**5** Valley fold the model in half, then rotate to the position shown. The open edge should be horizontal at the base, with the sharp point to the left.

**6** At the "toe", there is a triangular shape, with a raw edge that cuts across the model. Fold the lower edge of the large flap at the right (single layer only) upward, so that it now lies along this raw edge.

**7** On the same flap behind, there is a small triangular flap lying above a long thin section of napkin. Valley fold this triangle over, making a clean narrow strip of material at the back of the model.

**8** Wrap the entire section formed in step 7 forward, tightly around the "ankle" of the boot, and lock by tucking the end inside the pocket formed by the edges of the "toe" section (see step 6).

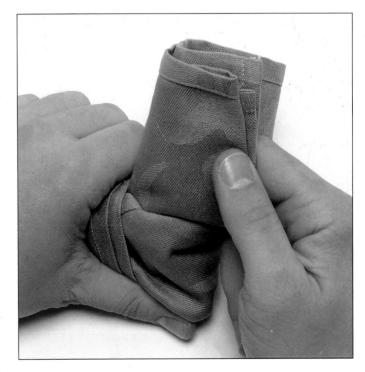

**9** Curve and shape the main body of the boot, pulling the upper part back to straighten it. Also flatten the toe slightly, which will help the model to stand better.

# swan napkin

While this napkin fold can be made from material napkins, a paper napkin works better. As a clever display idea, try sliding the chest of the swan between the central prongs of an upturned fork, which then lies across a plate holding the swan in place. The model is free-standing, however. Leave the serviette folded into quarters, straight from the packet.

**1** It is vital to begin with the corner where the four loose flaps of the napkin meet at the top, when the paper is arranged as a diamond, as shown. Fold in half, side to side, and unfold, to establish the vertical diagonal crease.

**2** Fold a Kite base. Note that the open end of the napkin is at the top, so it is opposite the corner you are folding to.

**3** Turn the napkin over, then fold the two long sides into the vertical centre line, thus narrowing the model to a sharp point. This is quite tricky to do since the layers underneath tend to slide out of place, so hold the napkin down firmly on to your folding surface as you do this, to keep all the layers together.

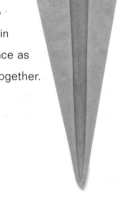

**4** Fold the sharp point up to the top.

**5** Fold the sharp point back down towards you by approximately a third of its length.

**6** Mountain-fold the model in half along the vertical centre line, then rotate to the position shown.

**7** Hold the body of the swan between finger and thumb of one hand, and the neck (the sharp point) between finger and thumb of the other hand. Slide the neck upwards, until it swings into a new position (not quite vertical, but sloping slightly to the rear). Flatten the model, pressing in the new crease at the base of the neck.

**8** Repeat this move with the head, holding the neck and the tip of the beak, and swivelling the head upwards slightly, forming a new crease.

**9** To fan out the tail feathers, hold the base of the swan's neck firmly between finger and thumb of one hand. Very carefully tease out the uppermost ply of the tissue at the tail end, pulling it upward until it forms a soft point lying along the rear edge of the neck. Don't be afraid to tease out the paper as far as it will comfortably go.

**10** Repeat step 9 with the next layer of tissue at the tail.

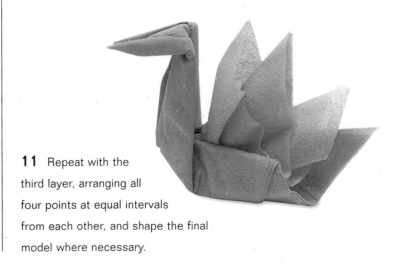

**11** Repeat with the third layer, arranging all four points at equal intervals from each other, and shape the final model where necessary.

# rose napkin

The creator of this design is unknown, but it is believed to have been collected by Stephen Weiss. Such party tricks and napkin folds are often taught to the young and passed on from one generation to the next. It is quite a tricky final technique to master, and, because you are using a tissue napkin, you will need to treat the material with great care.

**1** Begin with a tissue napkin, as square as it can possibly be (not all packet napkins are cut perfectly square). Open the napkin out completely, and arrange as shown.

**2** Fold the left edge inwards by 2–3cm/¾–1¼in.

**3** Now fold the lower edge up by 2–3cm/¾–1¼in.

**4** Place two fingers across the napkin, holding the horizontal strip at the lower left corner, using your thumb to hold the napkin underneath.

**5** Begin to roll the lower edge upward, doubling over the 2–3cm/¾–1¼in once again.

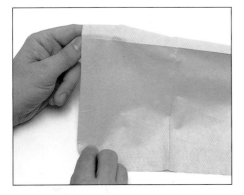

**6** To help you roll the entire height of the napkin, use your other hand to wrap the upper portion of the tissue over towards you, over the horizontal roll of material.

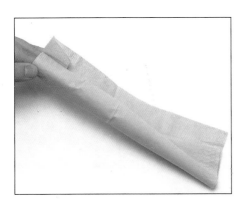

**7** The rolling almost completed.

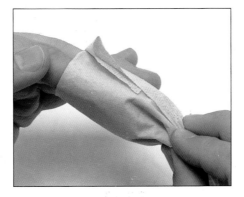

**8** About 4–5cm/1½–2in in from the left edge, pinch the tissue tightly, squeezing the layers flat, whilst allowing the left-hand section to remain loosely rolled.

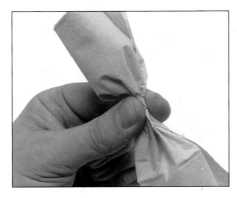

**9** Begin twisting the napkin tightly, to form the stem.

**10** Continue twisting to about halfway down the length of the roll.

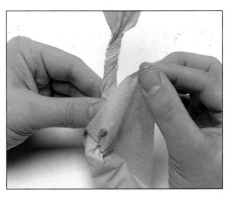

**11** Take hold of the outermost corner of the napkin at the lower end of the tube: the base of the stem. Pull this layer upward, fluffing the ply of tissue into a soft point.

**12** Continue twisting the lower end of the rose, to complete the stem.

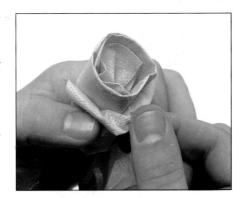

**13** For the rosebud, carefully turn the outer rolled layers over, to suggest the outer petals. Carefully arrange the inner rolled layers to suggest the inner petals.

# christmas stocking

This traditional model was originally a napkin fold, but has been adapted here to be made from conventional paper. The lock at the end ensures that the necessary layers of paper stay together. You will need a square of fairly crisp paper, not too thick, and preferably with a different colour on the reverse side. Fancy Christmas giftwrap works exceedingly well.

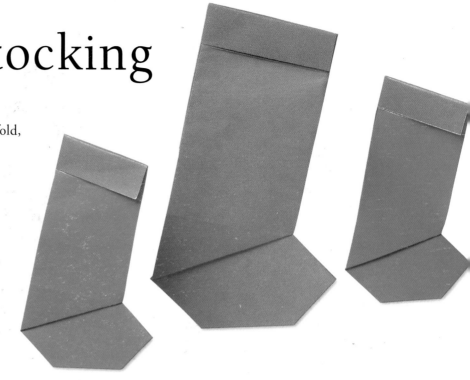

**1** With the colour you wish to be predominant in the design on top, fold up a narrow strip at the lower edge. A strip 1–2cm/½–¾in works fine with a square cut from A4 paper (21 x 29cm/8¼ x 11½in).

**2** Turn the paper over, then fold in half to establish the vertical centre crease. The strip folded in step 1 should be horizontal along the lower edge at this stage, even though it is hidden in the photograph.

**3** Rotate the paper 90° anticlockwise and fold the top and bottom sides to lie along the centre crease.

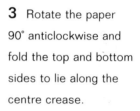

**4** Fold the left-hand corners inward to meet the centre crease.

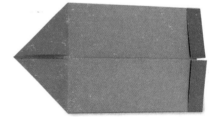

**5** Fold the left-hand corner across to meet the inner edges of the flaps folded in step 4.

**6** Fold this newly created edge across to the right-hand edge.

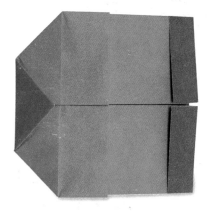

**7** Fold the upper layer back across to the left, making a vertical pleat in the paper. The outer corners of this section should come to rest on top of the right-angled corners beneath.

**8** Turn the model round so that the narrow strip lies at the top. Valley fold the model in half along the vertical centre crease, so that all the folds are inside. Hold as shown, with the finger and thumb of one hand close to the trim at the top, while the finger and thumb of the other grip the "toe".

**9** Swing the toe forward and outward, so that the pleat folded in steps 6–7 is allowed to stretch. New creases will form, and the toe will move position. Flatten the model.

**10** To lock the model, open out the two rear edges and look inside the Stocking. On one side only, carefully lift up the border folded in step 1, creating a pocket. Now refold the Stocking, this time tucking the upper corner of the remaining half into this pocket.

**11** Flatten the model to complete.

# gift tag

Animal models are very common in origami. They are often delightfully simple to produce and even design yourself. Indeed with this puppy, created by Paul Jackson, there are ample variations that can be conjured up just by altering one or two of the folds in the sequence. You will need two squares; the ideal size for a gift tag is, say, 7–8cm/2¾–3¼in square. One square should have a reverse colour, which can be used to suggest the nose.

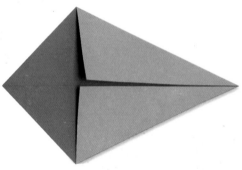

**1** Fold a Kite base for the body. You can use a square that is either duo coloured or the same on both sides, as from the opening folds, the colour you begin with face up will not be seen again. Arrange as shown.

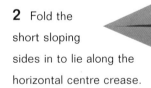

**2** Fold the short sloping sides in to lie along the horizontal centre crease.

**3** Fold the right-hand point across to meet the two flaps folded in step 2.

**4** Fold the upper sloping edge of the flap folded in step 3 back to the right again, so that this edge comes to rest along the right-hand vertical edge to make the tail.

**5** Turn the model over to complete the body. Rotate the paper 90° when making the final assembly.

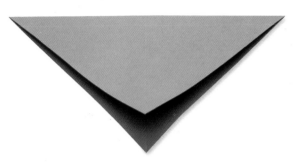

**6** For the head, fold the remaining square in half diagonally, the nose colour on the inside when beginning. Arrange so that the fold you have just made runs horizontally along the top.

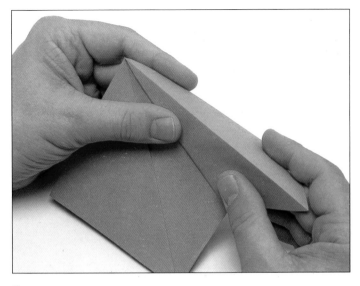

**9** Mountain fold the upper half of this squash fold behind on the hinge crease, to form the ear.

**10** Repeat steps 8–9 on the left side point.

**7** Fold both sharp points down to the right-angled corner.

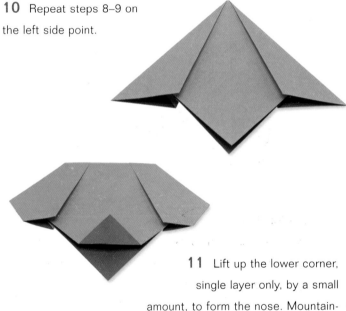

**8** Lift up the flap folded in step 7 (at the right) on the hinge crease, so that it projects upward perpendicular to the rest of the model. Symmetrically squash fold this point.

**11** Lift up the lower corner, single layer only, by a small amount, to form the nose. Mountain-fold the upper point behind to shape the head, and add further mountain folds at the outer edges of the ears.

**12** Attach the head to the body with a little glue. The completed puppy dog Gift Tag, ready to be attached to the present and addressed.

# pop-up flower

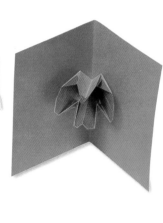

This model was designed by Jose Meeusen, and is a wonderful pop-up for the inside of a card. Ideally fold it from a fairly small square, say, 7–8cm/2¾–3¼in each side. It looks its best when folded from patterned paper.

**1** Begin with a Preliminary base, the inner colour being the inner colour of the opening flower. Have the model arranged like a diamond, with the open points at the top.

**2** Fold the single layer at the top down to the lower corner, pinch-creasing in the halfway mark, as a guide to the next fold.

**3** Fold the two side corners, single layer only, into the centre of the model.

**4** Fold the inner raw edges outward again to lie along the fold made in step 3.

**5** Repeat steps 3–4 on the reverse face.

**6** Unfold steps 3–5.

**7** Using existing creases, inside reverse fold each of the corners folded in the previous four steps firstly inward, then out again.

**8** Step 7 completed.

**9** Blunt the open corner by folding the single layer down by a small amount. Repeat on the reverse face.

**10** Fold the large flap at the right, single layer only across to the left using the natural vertical hinge crease. Repeat on the reverse side.

**11** Repeat step 9 on the remaining upper points, now in view.

**12** Place the flower as shown, against the spine crease of a card folded in half. Stick into place, applying the glue only to the small triangular area close to the base of the flower.

**13** Apply glue to the upper side of the flower, as shown.

**14** Fold the card in half, left to right, so that the flower is sandwiched in-between the layers. Carefully press flat.

**15** Wait for the glue to dry. Open the card, and the flower pops up. The finished Pop-up Flower.

# button flower

Gay Merrill Gross has a wonderful talent for designing simple elegant folds, like this Button Flower, which, like the name implies, should be folded small enough so that it can be attached to the button of a garment, as a decoration. It can also make an attractive page marker to a book, or brighten up the corner of a letter. Three squares of fairly thin, crisp paper are required, two of identical size, one two-thirds the size of the other two.

**1** Begin by pre-creasing the centre line of one of the larger squares, then fold two opposite edges to the centre. The colour you begin with uppermost will be the colour of the outer petals.

**3** Crease in the two diagonals.

**2** Unfold step 1 completely. Rotate the paper so that the creases already made are vertical, and then repeat step 1, making new creases in the other direction.

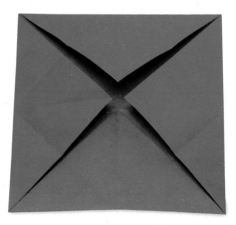

**4** Turn the paper over, and Blintz fold the four corners to the centre.

**5** Unfold step 4. Turn the paper back over, then fold any two adjacent outer edges to the central creases simultaneously, allowing the paper at the corner to create a point.

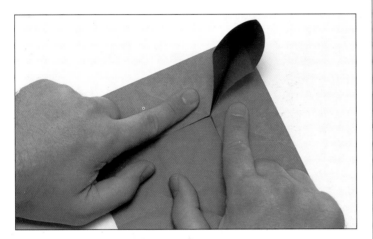

**6** Step 5 in progress.

**7** Open and squash the raised point down, forming a half-Preliminary base.

**8** Repeat all the way around the model, allowing the outer edges already folded in to swing outward on the Blintz creases formed in step 4.

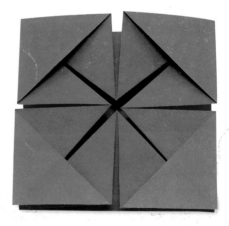

**9** Fold all the four inner raw corners outward. Outer section completed.

**10** Repeat steps 1–9 with the smaller square. Begin attaching the two completed parts of the model together, by inserting all four corners of the inner section into those of the outer section.

**11** Step 10 in progress.

**12** Step 10 completed. Pull out the four raw corners of the inner section, so that they lie on top of the outer petals (see the final photograph).

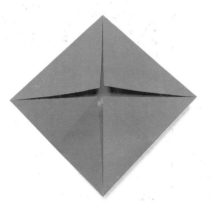

**13** Take the last sheet of paper, and, after folding in half in both directions corner to corner, to establish the two diagonal creases, Blintz fold the four corners to the centre.

**14** Turn the paper over, and Blintz fold the upper and lower corners to the centre.

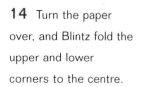

**15** Attach the leaf and completed flower sections together in a similar way to how you joined the two flower sections in steps 10–12.

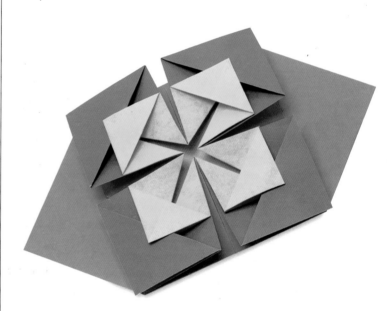

**16** The completed Button Flower. To attach to a button on a garment, slide the button under the loose corners underneath the model, so that each of the Blintz folds slips behind the button and holds the model in place. For a page marker or letter corner, at step 14 simply leave one of the secondary blintz folds undone, slide the model on to the corner via the slots at the back, then refold the remaining blintzed corner as one with the page, locking as previously shown, so that the model is securely attached.

# paperchain

So many models look as if they have been waiting around for years to be created; they appear almost too obvious not to have been thought of before. This design, an idea by Laura Kruskal, is a case in point, where two simple units are joined to make the square link of a chain. Other units are interlocked with the first, to produce a garland paperchain.

**1** Fold and unfold a 2:1 rectangle of paper in half, bringing the two longest sides together, to establish the horizontal centre crease, then fold the two outer long edges to the centre.

**2** Rotate the paper by 90°, then fold and unfold in half to determine the centre crease. Fold the two short edges to the centre.

**3** Mountain-fold the model in half along the long centre line, arranging it as shown.

**4** Take hold of the left portion of the paper between a finger and thumb of your left hand. With your right hand, take hold of the end of the right-hand strip, lying along the upper edge. Begin to pull this section upwards.

**5** Swivel it into a new position at 90° to the rest of the model. Flatten the model.

**6** Repeat steps 4–5 at the left-hand end of the model to make a completed unit. Make a second unit the same way.

**7** To join units, carefully open out the inner raw edges (folded in step 1) of one unit, and slide the end of the other unit underneath these edges.

**8** Interlock several links by repeating step 7 with the remaining open ends of the two units.

# heart ring

Designed by Hiroshi Kumasaka, this elegant model can be made as a napkin ring, or in miniature to fit a finger. There is a very simple yet effective use of the reverse colour here, so, if making a finger ring, duo paper which is gold on one side and red on the other would be ideal. Foil works very well. Experiment with paper sizes for whatever kind of ring you require; the length of one side of the starting square will be roughly the circumference of the ring, with an allowance for the overlap to lock.

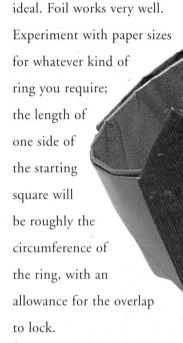

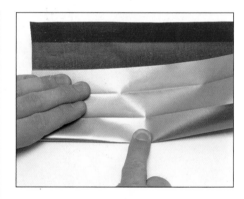

**1** Begin with the heart-colour side facing you. We are about to divide the paper horizontally into eighths. First of all fold and unfold the halfway crease, then pre-crease the quarter creases by bringing upper and lower edges to the centre, and once again unfolding.

**2** Fold and unfold the upper and lower edges to the first quarter crease in each case.

**3** Fold and unfold the upper and lower edges to the opposite side quarter crease (now appearing as the second crease away from the opposite raw edge).

**4** You have now divided the paper into eight equal horizontal bands. Fold the paper in half, side to side, to establish the vertical centre line. Unfold again.

**5** Turn the paper over, and fold down one eighth strip along the top.

**6** Turn the paper back over once more, and fold the upper corners down to lie along the vertical centre line.

**7** Turn the paper over once more, and fold the upper point down to meet the third crease from the top.

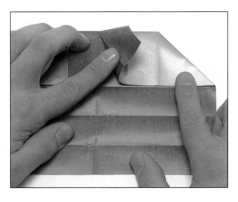

**8** Turn the paper back over once more. You are now going to make a swivel and a squash fold. Push upward and outward on the vertical folded edge of the inner coloured border, sliding outwards until it comes to lie along the upper horizontal edge behind. Do this on both sides.

**9** Step 8 completed.

**10** Fold the flaps down once more, bringing the short horizontal edges along the top to lie along the vertical centre line.

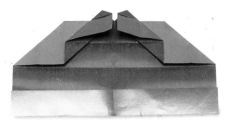

**11** Fold up a one eighth strip at the bottom.

**12** Double this edge over three more times. The horizontal band formed will be quite thick now. It helps to fold very carefully each time you double the paper over, aiming to position the edge just short of the next crease line up, to avoid getting uneven and messy layering.

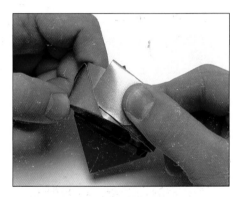

**13** Take hold of each end of the model, and curve it into a ring, tucking one end into the pocket created by the diagonal folded edge on the outside of the other end. Push in as far as it will comfortably go, then round and shape the model between your fingers; this curved tension will help to hold the ring together.

# star

This is a wonderful Christmas star invented by Martin Wall which uses the crease pattern of the Bird base. An effective way to make a card using this design is to mount several stars on top of each other, each offset to the one before, and attached to a piece of card the same colour; this will create a relief effect. For the model use a square of thin, crisp paper with the star colour face down to start.

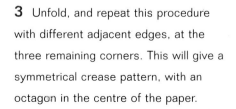

**2** Fold a Kite base with any two adjacent edges.

**1** Begin by folding the paper diagonally in half in both directions, folding and unfolding each time, marking the diagonals with creases.

**3** Unfold, and repeat this procedure with different adjacent edges, at the three remaining corners. This will give a symmetrical crease pattern, with an octagon in the centre of the paper.

**4** Turn the paper over, and fold in half, bottom to top.

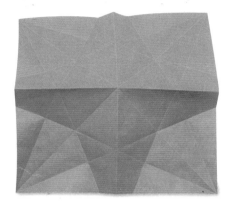

**5** Unfold, and then fold in half, side to side, at right angles to the crease you have just made. Unfold, then turn the paper over so that the original side is uppermost, and the diagonals and Bird-base creases are all valley folds.

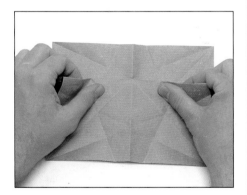

**6** Grasp the horizontal central mountain fold between fingers and thumbs. Drag it away from you, until you can rest the entire folded edge on the intersection of the upper Bird-base creases and the vertical halfway line. Press flat, creating a pleat across the paper.

**7** Step 6 completed.

**8** Rotate the paper, so that the pleat made in step 6 is now vertical, and the thinner portion of the paper lies to the right. Again, grasp the horizontal crease across the centre of the paper, sliding it once more away from you, until you can place it down where the folded edge of the pleat made in step 6 intersects with the uppermost Bird-base creases. You will now have a perfect, small square in the top right corner. Flatten the model.

**9** From now on, we only use existing creases. Starting with one outside edge of the larger square, refold on the Kite-base creases, allowing the adjacent flap to swivel and squash into place at the same time.

**10** Step 9 completed and rotated.

**11** Repeat step 9 all the way around, forming the remaining three points of the star.

# santa and sleigh

There are origami societies all over the world, each producing its own magazine. This model, by Sanae Sakai, was featured in the Nippon Origami Society of Japan's December 1996 issue. Use a square of paper, preferably red on one side. Begin with this side face up.

**1** Begin by folding the paper in half, left to right, and making a pinch-mark along the upper edge.

**2** Unfold, then fold the paper across once more, to meet with the pinch made in step 1. Pinch again, down to about a quarter of the way from the top edge.

**3** Unfold step 2.

**4** Fold the upper left-hand corner down to lie along the pinch made in step 2.

**5** Turn the paper over, arranging the folded corner to be top right.

**6** Again using the pinch made in step 2 as a guide, fold the right-hand edge inward so that, at the top, the edge lies along the pinch.

**7** Fold the top edge down on a crease which runs horizontally in line with the lower edge of the tiny triangular section in step 6.

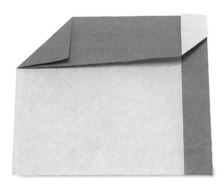

**8** Fold the top left corner down to the raw edge of the flap folded in step 7.

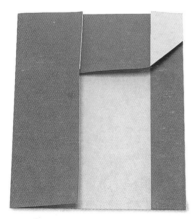

**9** Using this triangular flap (now hidden) as your guide, fold the left-hand vertical edge inward, on a crease which runs along the inner edge. Release and unfold the triangular flap folded in step 8.

**10** Allowing this side flap to unfold slightly, pull out the hidden corner, stretching the excess paper to a point.

**11** Step 10 in progress.

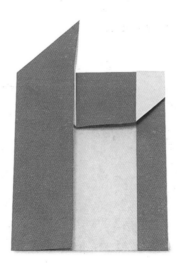

**12** Step 10 completed. This particular type of swivel move occurs frequently in this model.

**13** Raise the point created in steps 10–12 so that it stands up perpendicular to the rest of the model.

**14** Squash fold this flap into a half-Preliminary base. Also fold up the lower right corner to the inner edge of the vertical strip.

**15** Similar to step 9, fold the lower edge up, over the tiny triangular flap folded in step 14, creating a horizontal parallel border along the bottom. Again, release and unfold the triangular flap. Unfold triangular flap from step 14. ▶

**16** At the lower right corner, once again pull out the hidden point, squashing outward to the right.

**17** At the lower left corner, perform a similar swivel, this time noting that the vertical border is wider than the horizontal border.

**18** The effect will be as shown.

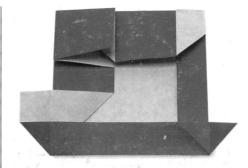

**19** Step 17 completed. All edges should be at right angles to each other.

**20** Fold the inner lower corner of the Preliminary base up to the top. Also fold the raw corner at the left down to meet the horizontal border along the bottom.

**21** Unfold the first fold made at step 20, then fold the inner corner back up to the crease line made in step 20.

**22** To make the trim on Santa's hat, double the lower edge of the flap folded in step 21 over.

**23** Then double the edge over once more.

**24** Lift up the upper right section of paper, and fold the inner raw edge of the horizontal border upwards, to lie along the outer edge of what will be Santa's face.

**25** Allow the right-hand vertical border to double over once more.

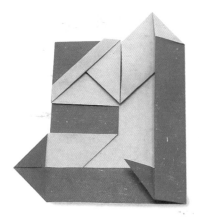

**26** Step 25 completed. Flatten the model.

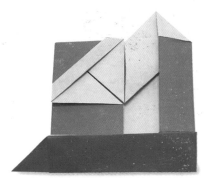

**27** Fold the lower edge up once more, doubling the horizontal border over, as shown.

**28** Pull out the hidden point (the front blade of the sleigh) at the lower right corner, and swivel and slide into position, much the same way as you have done previously in this model.

**29** Step 28 completed.

**30** Mountain fold the model diagonally in half, the crease running top left to bottom right. This fold is made quite naturally, the thing to remember is not to fold the front of the sleigh section, or the right side (as you look) of Santa's face.

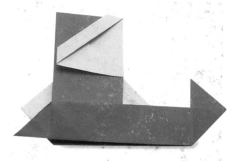

**31** Step 30 completed.

**32** Add shaping mountain folds to the rear corner of the sleigh, the sides of Santa's face, and Santa's toy bag.

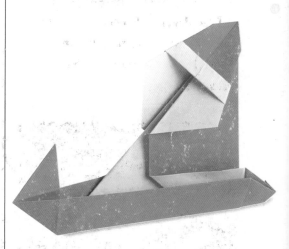

**ABOVE** The completed Santa and Sleigh

# Modular Origami

Modular origami, which has been increasing in
popularity for the last 20 years, breaks the rules of
pure origami by combining several identical pieces
to create one spectacular model. It is nearly always
the case that creating the units is far less
problematic than putting the final model together,
which often requires much patience and practice.

# spinner

One of many wonderful designs by the late Lewis Simon, this model combines two standard bases, the Waterbomb base and the Preliminary base, to form a rigid modular construction. Use 12 sheets of fairly sturdy paper. The outer colour of the entire model will be the same as the outer colour of the Preliminary bases.

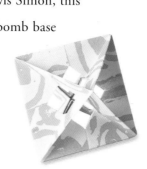

**1** Fold six Waterbomb and six Preliminary bases. Open out one of each base slightly, and allow the Preliminary base to wrap around the outside of the Waterbomb base, lining up the creases in the two bases.

**3** Allow the Waterbomb base to reform, the two sheets folded as one. Repeat for the remaining bases.

**5** In the same way, join adjacent points of the first two units into similar points of a third unit, forming a triangular section in the centre, as shown.

**2** Mountain fold each of the four corners of the Preliminary base inward, over the outer raw edges of the Waterbomb base, locking the sheets of paper together.

**4** Join any two units together by slipping the raw (Waterbomb) point of the first unit over the raw point of the other, but underneath the raw edge created by the Preliminary base. Push in all the way, until the two edges of what were the Preliminary bases meet.

**6** Add the final units in the same way; the last unit is the most difficult to add. To activate the model place the points of the completed spinner into the centre of your open palms, holding firmly. Blow hard against the top point of the model, and the spinner will really spin.

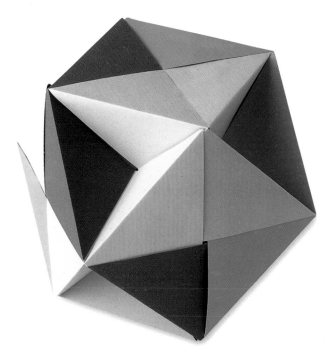

# butterfly ball

This apparently solid geometric shape, designed by Kenneth Kawamura, can be hit open-handed in mid-air, where it explodes, cascading colourful butterflies everywhere. A shallow square box can be used to help support the sides of the Butterfly Ball while you add more units. Use 12 squares of fairly heavyweight paper.

**1** Fold a Waterbomb base then pull open the front and rear faces. The angle along the lower edge (inside the model), where adjacent points meet, should be a right angle. Make 11 more units.

**2** Place a unit, triangle side down, on to your folding surface. Place a second unit inside the first at 90° to it so that half of the triangle overlaps. Connect with two more units so that the triangular faces form an interwoven pattern at the base.

**3** Each side of the Butterfly Ball will appear the same, so, when adding the next tier of units, turn each of the four waterbomb bases around, so that the points are projecting upwards and downwards. As you slot each unit into place at the corners, make sure that once again you interweave the points over and under, so that the model will hold together at the end. In each lower corner inside the ball, there is a triangular construction of three units; make sure that each one lies both over and under its neighbour.

**4** The second tier of units all added.

**5** Add the third and final tier of units in the same way. You will complete a four-unit weave on top in just the same way as you started at the base. Have patience as you add the last 2–3 units. The completed Butterfly Ball. To burst the model: throw it gently into the air. As it descends, use the palm of your hand to smack the ball back upward. The ball will open in a spray of colour, as the butterflies shower to the ground.

# Japanese brocade

This design, by Minako Ishibashi, makes attractive earrings, when folded from extremely small squares, say 4 x 4cm/1½ x 1½in. For a practice version, begin with six squares of fairly sturdy paper. This modular design is very original, featuring curved surfaces, which seem to create the illusion of rings encircling the central cube shape. Only one colour shows on the finished unit, so begin with this colour face down. Two squares each of three different colours can also be used, as here.

**1** Begin by folding the square in half in one direction, to establish the centre line. Fold upper and lower edges in to meet this crease.

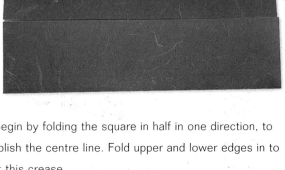

**2** Fold the right vertical edge upward on a diagonal crease to lie along the upper edge. Fold the left vertical edge downward to lie on the lower edge. This forms a parallelogram.

**3** Unfold the paper completely.

**4** Fold all four corners inward to lie on the horizontal quarter creases. Two of these creases will already have been made.

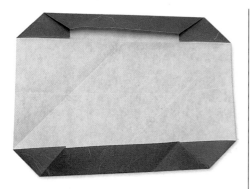

**5** Fold the upper and lower edges in to lie along the horizontal quarter creases.

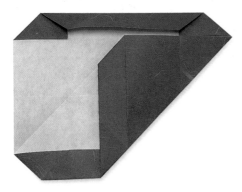

**6** Fold the lower right flap inward on the existing crease, made in step 2.

**7** Peel back the inner vertical edge of the flap folded in step 6, on an existing parallel crease, while at the same time folding up the lower edge, also on the existing crease. This performs both a swivel and a squash fold.

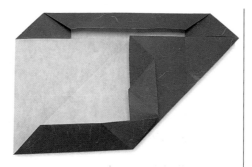

**8** Step 7 completed.

**9** Repeat steps 6–7 for the top left flap.

**10** Pull out the lower border, and allow the flap folded in step 9 to tuck in behind it. Flatten the model once more.

**11** Step 10 completed.

**12** Turn the model over, and fold each of the sharp points to the obtuse angles of the parallelogram, as shown.

**13** Allow the flaps folded in step 12 to be unfolded slightly, to rest at right angles to the central square shape. Make five more identical units.

▶

**14** To assemble, slide the point of any one unit under the central section of another unit, as shown.

**15** Continue by adding a third unit, assembling the central cube piece by piece. If folding with two units of three different colours, you should add units of the same colour opposite each other. All the units are joined in the same way, all the way around the model.

**16** Under construction.

**17** Assembly finished.

**18** Finally, squeeze together the four flaps that appear on each of the six faces of the central cube, allowing them to project upward slightly and form the circular "bands" around the model.

**RIGHT** The completed Japanese Brocade.

# five intersecting tetrahedra

This ingenious design was devised by Tom Hull, using a unit created by Francis Ow. The original form was a simple tetrahedron: a skeletal frame made from six individual struts. Tom found a way of interweaving five tetrahedra to create the final masterpiece shown. This is a highly complex model to assemble, and it is important to understand just how the units are interwoven. To assist you, the final steps show stages of two tetrahedra, three tetrahedra, four tetrahedra and finally the intersecting five modular constructions. Use ten squares of fairly stiff paper, ideally two sheets of five different colours. Divide each square into thirds by folding, then trim down the fold lines, yielding three 1 : 3 strips. You will eventually have 30 strips of paper, ready to fold the model. This model can also be made from US dollar notes.

**1** Begin with the strip positioned horizontally lengthways. The colour on top to begin with will not show on the final model. Fold the paper in half, bringing the two longest sides together, to establish the horizontal centre crease. Unfold. Then fold upper and lower edges to the centre line.

**2** Pick up the model from your folding surface. At the far end, fold the right folded edge into the centre, but pinch-crease only, creasing 3–4cm/1¼ x 1½in down from the short upper edge.

**3** Fold the upper left-hand corner across to the right, so that it comes to rest upon the pinch-crease made in step 2. The crease you are now making also connects with the centre of the short upper edge.

**6** Open out step 3 (the left corner) and begin to inside reverse fold the corner inwards on existing creases. This step shows the move in progress.

**9** Using the crease made in step 4, double over the outer edge at the right.

**10** Repeat steps 2–10 at the other end of the strip. Once again, begin by pinch-creasing the right side, so that the little inside reverse folds are formed at opposite corners.

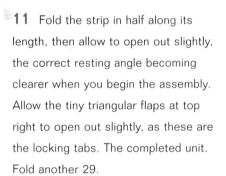

**4** Fold the upper right-hand corner over the edge of the small triangle created in step 3, which will make the two sides equal in the angle, and amount of corner folded.

**7** Step 6 completed.

**11** Fold the strip in half along its length, then allow to open out slightly, the correct resting angle becoming clearer when you begin the assembly. Allow the tiny triangular flaps at top right to open out slightly, as these are the locking tabs. The completed unit. Fold another 29.

**8** At the right corner, fold the upper horizontal edge down to meet the crease made in step 4.

**5** Open out step 4.

**12** Turn each unit over, so that as you lock them together, you are looking at the outside (the smooth face) of the paper. Lock any two units by carefully sliding the small triangular tab on one unit into the slit pocket (the inside reverse fold made in steps 6–7) of the other.

**13** Step 12 completed. See how the units fit flush together, so that they sit at the correct angle to which further units can be joined.

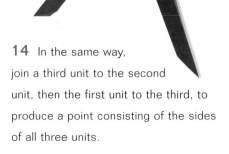

**14** In the same way, join a third unit to the second unit, then the first unit to the third, to produce a point consisting of the sides of all three units.

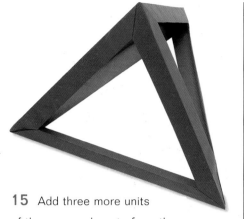

**15** Add three more units of the same colour, to form the single tetrahedron.

**16** The finished tetrahedron from a slightly different angle, showing the construction. When adding further tetrahedra, you will need to leave some corners open until you have interwoven the separate constructions correctly. Only then can you make the locking connections.

**17** Tom Hull's advice on how to add the completed tetrahedra is that there is a very strong symmetry behind the formation of this structure, and understanding this symmetry can aid you in the construction. The finished object should have the following property: any two tetrahedra are interwoven with one corner poking through a hole in the other, and vice versa, like a three-dimensional Star of David, but slightly twisted.

**18** Three tetrahedra interwoven.

**19** Four tetrahedra interwoven.

**20** The completed Five Intersecting Tetrahedra.

# modular star

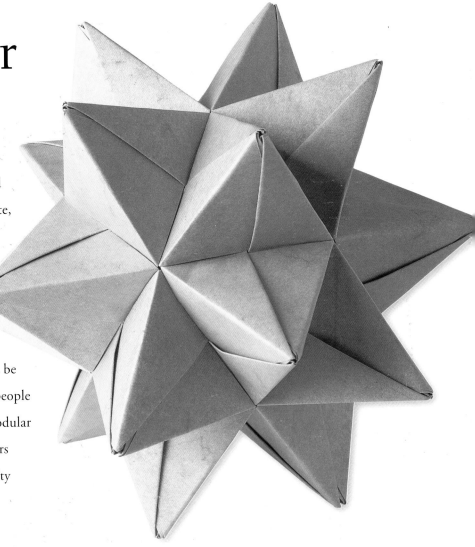

One of the most prolific origami authors is the Japanese expert Tomoko Fuse, who is most famous for her decorative multi-piece boxes and modular stars. This star has long been a favourite, and you should find the assembly fairly straightforward. The units themselves, 30 in total, are also quite easy to realize. Use sturdy paper with the same colour both sides, as trying to work out an appropriate colour sequence with the final construction can be quite a challenge in itself. Furthermore, many people feel that this works better since it allows the modular piece to be seen as a whole; lots of bright colours can sometimes distract the eye from its simplicity and elegance.

**1** Arrange the paper as a diamond shape, then fold and unfold the paper in half in both directions, bringing outer edges together. Pre-crease the vertical diagonal.

**2** Fold the lower corner up so that it meets with the halfway fold currently running lower left edge to upper right edge. The crease you are going to make ends at the right corner. This is quite tricky, because the crease approaches the right corner at a very acute angle, so fold carefully.

**3** You are now going to swivel and squash fold the paper. On the flap created in step 2, pinch the crease that was originally the diagonal into a mountain fold, swivelling the point across to lie on the vertical crease line beneath.

**4** Step 3 in progress.

**5** Step 3 completed. Repeat steps 3–4 on the upper corner. Flatten the model.

**6** Fold the lower right sloping edge upward to lie along the vertical centre crease.

**7** Running underneath the inner edge of the flap folded in step 6, there is a very narrow strip, which forms a pocket. Tuck the small triangular point created by the swivel in steps 3–4 into the pocket beneath this narrow edge.

**8** Carefully pull the flap folded in step 6 across to the right, just to make sure that it is locked in place, and is not allowed to slide.

**9** Steps 7–8 completed. Repeat steps 6–8 with the neighbouring flap.

**10** Turn the model over. Fold the second shortest side across to lie on the long side.

**11** Repeat at the other end. The outline of the model should be a diamond shape.

**12** Turn the model over, and fold in half, bringing the two sharp points together. Allow to unfold.

▶

**13** Allow the flaps folded in steps 10-11 to open out slightly, completing the unit, which now appears three-dimensional. Make another 29 units in the same way.

**14** Take any two units. Slide the point of one unit into the central slit in the diamond-shaped face of the other.

**15** Two units assembled.

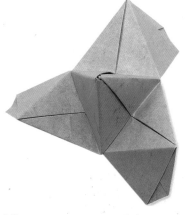

**16** Assemble a three-unit cluster, by adding a third unit in the same way. You will now also need to connect the third unit to the first. This requires swivelling the construction into position to allow these locks to be performed.

**BELOW** The completed Modular Star.

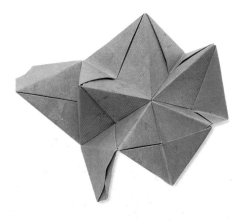

**17** When more units are added, you will notice that a ring of any five points forms a pentagonal star, as shown.

**18** Near to completion. Continue to lock the units as before.

# modular cube

One of several variations along a similar theme, this 12-piece modular cube by Lewis Simon is a favourite. The units are very simple to fold, the construction slightly more challenging; you slot points into pockets, with the middle section of each unit making up the principal part of two adjacent sides, while the ends of each unit fold around right-angled corners to lock the model together. Ideally use duo paper, beginning with the same side facing upward each time.

**1** Begin by dividing into thirds horizontally.

**2** Refold the lower third.

**3** Fold the raw edge of the third folded in step 2 back down to the lower edge. ▶

**4** Unfold step 3.

**5** Fold the raw edge once more, this time halfway, to the crease made in step 3.

**6** Double the folded edge created in step 5 over once more, giving an extra thickness to the long, thin horizontal strip.

**7** Repeat steps 2–6 on the upper portion of the paper.

**8** Using a diagonal crease, fold the right-hand vertical edge downward, to lie along the lower horizontal edge. At the left, fold the outer edge away from you to the upper edge. You will have a parallelogram.

**9** Unfold step 8.

**10** Refold step 8, allowing the triangular flap at the left to tuck in underneath the horizontal border strip on the upper portion of the paper.

**11** Flatten the model.

**12** Repeat steps 10–11 at the right.

**13** Turn the model over.

**14** Make folds at each end, so that the small, reverse-colour triangles are folded in half diagonally.

**15** Unfold step 14.

**16** Valley fold the model across the centre, bringing the shortest sides of the parallelogram together; the two obtuse angles will meet by this fold.

**17** Partially open out step 16, so that there is a right angle between the two sides of the unit. Make a further 11 units.

**18** Slot a second unit into the first, by the method shown: the end tab goes under the long, thin central border, pushes in until it folds around the angle to the adjacent side, and locks into place.

**19** Step 18 in progress.

**20** Add a third unit, locking by the same method. The tab on the third unit is then slotted into the "pocket" of the first unit, thus creating a triangular, truncated corner.

**21** Step 20 completed.

**22** Continue adding further units in the same way.

**LEFT** The completed Modular Cube is best displayed standing on one of the truncated corners.

# kusudama

A kusudama is a decorative modular ball. You can either fold it from paper you prepare yourself, or from kits that you can buy, which also include instructions and a beautiful tassel and loop by which to hang your finished model. Here, 30 squares of paper are required. Unlike many modular designs, the assembly of the units is made by slotting points into pockets on the inside of the model. This makes it a very complicated model to assemble, and patience will be needed.

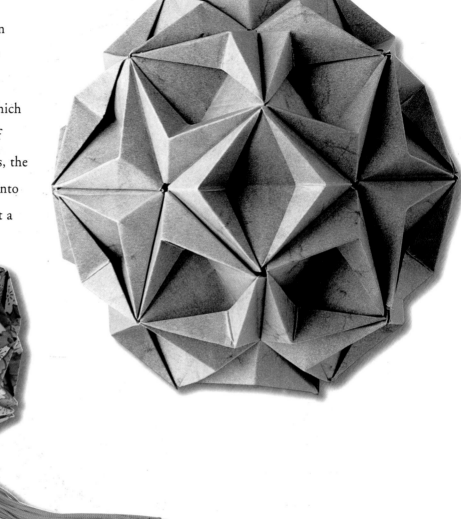

**1** Begin by folding and unfolding your first square in half, to establish the horizontal centre crease. Fold upper and lower edges to the centre.

**2** Using 45° diagonal folds, bring the right edge up to lie along the upper edge. Fold the left edge down to lie along the lower edge. This forms a parallelogram.

**3** Unfold step 2, and turn the paper over. Note the position of the creases made in step 2. Pre-crease the vertical centre line by folding in half, side to side, and unfolding.

**4** Repeat step 2 on this side.

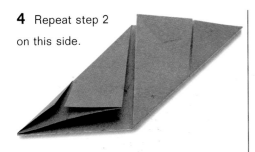

**5** Unfold step 4.

**6** Fold the outer edges to the centre.

**8** Unfold step 7, then bring the lower edge up to meet the diagonal crease on the right made in step 2 (now appearing as soft mountain folds). Again pinch-crease, this time from the lower right-hand corner to the vertical crease, which halves the right-hand section of the model. This pinch-crease, and the one made in step 7, will form a V shape.

**11** Repeat steps 7–10 on the upper left section of the model. Turn the model 180° to do this. Allow the model to unfold as shown.

**12** Refold the diagonal creases made in step 4.

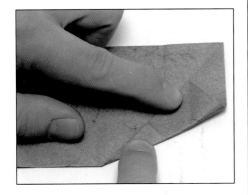

**7** Unfold step 6. Fold the right half of the lower edge up to meet with the diagonal fold made in step 4. Pinch-crease only from the lower edge to halfway across the right-hand panel, so that the crease you are now making meets with the vertical crease made in step 6.

**9** As you refold the vertical crease made in step 6, allow this V shape to form an inside reverse fold, as you collapse the paper.

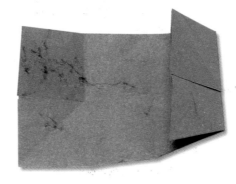

**10** Step 9 completed.

**13** Using a crease that lies beneath the central diamond shape, collapse the paper in half. The diamond will look like a mouth closing. Flatten the model to make good strong creases throughout, then allow to open up slightly.

▶

**14** Firmly crease the fold line that cuts across the outer points, forming little triangular flaps at each end of the unit. The Unit complete. Make 29 more.

**15** Turn the first unit over, so that you are looking at the reverse face. Take a second unit, and assemble as shown: the point of the second unit goes into the slit at the rear of the first unit.

**16** Step 15 completed. Allow the form to remain three-dimensional.

**17** Joining three units: take a third unit, and assemble as before, tucking the point into the slit at the rear of the second unit.

**18** Now join the third unit to the first, forming a point on the underside, while a triangular cavity appears face up. You will have to swivel the units into the correct position to make this possible.

**19** Steps 17–18 in progress.

**20** Three units joined.

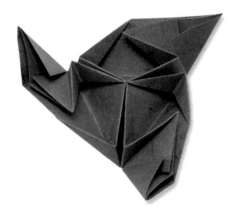

**21** Three units joined, the outside view.

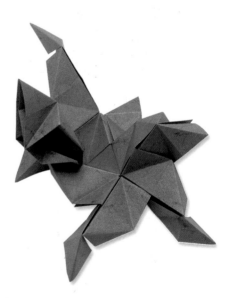

**22** Keep adding further units as before. At this point it is helpful to look at the illustration of the final model: see how five of the "mouth" formations of the original unit circle around to form a pentagonal star shape.

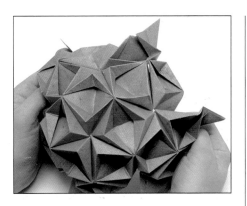

**23** The Star shape. This will be the outer face of the Kusudama. You may find it helpful to use a shallow box lid, approximately the size of the opening spread of ten or so units. The edges will support the side units as they are assembled, allowing the Kusudama to form into a three-dimensional shape without the weight of individual units pulling themselves and the others out of the locking position.

**26** More units added. You can use a paper clip to hold units together while you add the final ones, if you like.

**27** Adding the final units. You must make sure each pocket is ready to receive a point. It helps to hollow the pocket out with a sharp tool just prior to locking, and also make sure that the points are sharply folded, and lie at the right angle to simply slot in. This is a very complicated assembly procedure, so accept it as a challenge.

**BELOW** The completed Kusudama.

**24** More units added.

**25** More units added.

# fireworks

There are many examples in origami of what we call Flexagons, often multi-piece, where the final model can rotate and flex, producing a kaleidoscope effect. This one, designed by Yami Yamauchi, was the highlight of the International Origami Convention held by OUSA (Origami USA) a few years ago. The units are very easy to make, the construction slightly more difficult, especially the last two units. Use 12 squares of fairly crisp, strong paper. This is an extremely enjoyable model to fold, and great fun to play around with when completed.

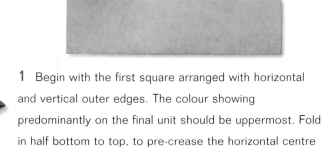

**1** Begin with the first square arranged with horizontal and vertical outer edges. The colour showing predominantly on the final unit should be uppermost. Fold in half bottom to top, to pre-crease the horizontal centre line. Fold upper and lower edges to this crease line.

**2** Unfold step 1, turn the paper over, then fold and unfold in half diagonally in both directions.

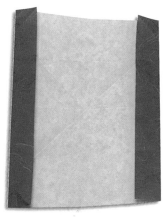

**3** With the quarter creases remaining horizontal, as shown, fold the left and right edges inward to meet with the intersection of the outer quarter and diagonal pre-creases. Crease firmly here.

**4** Unfold step 3, then form a Waterbomb base allowing the diagonals to fold naturally as valley creases.

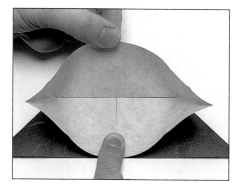

**5** Lift up the lower edge, single layer only, so that it meets the upper point.

**6** Then squash the flap into a kind of tent shape (the point of the Waterbomb base comes to rest at the centre of the lower edge).

**7** Step 6 completed.

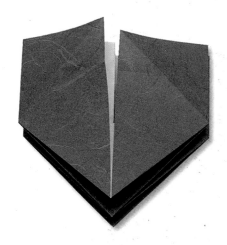

**8** Repeat steps 5–7 on the reverse face, then rotate the paper 180° into the position shown.

**9** Fold the upper raw edge, single layer only, down on the creases made in step 3. To be able to flatten the model, you will need to allow a small triangular-shaped squash fold to form at the upper corners.

**10** Repeat on the adjacent flap, and on the reverse face.

**11** Unfold steps 9–10. The completed unit. Fold 11 more.

►

**12** Each unit consists of four large flaps, two to the right, and two to the left of the model. There is also a slit down the vertical centre of each unit, with a pocket behind. The vertical centre crease can be used to fold the flaps over from one side of the model to the other. Opening out the two pockets on the first unit, slide in the rear flaps of the second unit.

**13** This shows the right side being worked on.

**14** The first two units together.

**15** Fold one large flap at the left across to the right, using the vertical centre crease. Parts of both units will be folded across as one.

**16** Refold the squash-fold arrangements made originally in steps 9–10.

**17** Now turn the paper over, and fold two flaps across from right to left.

**18** Repeat step 16.

**19** Turn the layers so that once again everything is symmetrical, and there are an equal number of large flaps to the right and left. The upper layer will look something like a heart, as the upper corners of this unit will now be missing.

**20** Continue adding more units in the same way.

**21** All twelve units added. Now, to join the last unit to the first, very carefully swing both ends around into a ring. Even more carefully (so that the previously locked units do not come apart) tuck the units together, then make the necessary squash folds to complete the model.

**RIGHT** The completed Fireworks.

## HOW TO USE

Hold carefully with each palm, so that your fingers are underneath, and the model is cupped in your hands. Hold firmly, and push up with your fingers from underneath. The central section will rise towards you, and Fireworks will be able to flex into a different form. This process can be repeated again and again.

# acknowledgements

I wish to acknowledge and thank all the many paperfolders throughout the world who have been an inspiration to me since my childhood, far too many to list by name. And to everyone I have ever met who has shared my joy of origami with me, my gratitude indeed.

The author and publisher would like to thank everyone who contributed their origami designs to this book, specifically the origamists who are responsible for the projects and the wonderful creations featured in the Gallery section:

Sanny Ang pp117-119; Angela Baldo p18; Paulo Bascetta pp60-63; Jeff Beynon p22; Ruthanne Bessman p20; Alfred Bestall pp78-79; David Brill pp22-23, 60-63; Adolfo Cerceda pp102-109; Rae Cooker pp182-183; Edwin Corrie pp86-89; Nobuyoshi Enomoto pp96-101; Vincent Floderer pp169-171; Tomoko Fuse pp138-143, 199, 238-240; Alice Gray pp56-57, 73-75; Alfredo Giunta p19; Andrew Hans p18; Robert Harbin pp49, 52; Larry Hart pp154-155; Tom Hull pp235-237; Prof. Humiaki Huzita pp158-159; Minako Ishibashi pp232-234; Paul Jackson pp68-69, 73-75, 122-123, 128-130, 187-189, 212-213; Eric Joisel p21; Kunihiko Kasahara p66-68, 90-95; Kenneth Kawamura p231; Toshikazu Kawasaki p19; Eric Kenneway pp148-149, 166-168; Ulrike Krallmann-Wenzel p116; Laura Kruskal p219; Hiroshi Kumasaka pp220-221; Michael LaFosse pp115, 146; Robert Lang pp20, 134-137; Soon Young Lee pp184-186; Jose Meeusen pp214-215; David Mitchell, pp14, 21; Robert Neale pp72, 124-125; Masamichi Noma pp82-85; Francis Ow; pp160-162; Chris Palmer p22; Aldo Putignano pp163-165; Sam Randlett pp128-130; Sanae Sakai pp224-227; Jeremy Shafer pp180-181; Lewis Simon pp230, 241-243; Ed Sullivan pp178-179; Toshie Takahama pp90-95; Florence Temko pp76-77; Teruo Tsuji pp131-133; Kosho Uchiyama pp120-121; Martin Wall pp222-223; Stephen Weiss pp208-209; Makoto Yamaguchi pp126-127; Yami Yamauchi pp248-251; Akira Yoshizawa p19

PICTURE CREDITS:
Express Newspapers p6(l)
Robin Macey pp6(r), 7, 11(l), 12(t), 14(t&b)
Rick Beech p13
Kelly-Mooney/Corbis p15 (l)

## Paper suppliers

UNITED KINGDOM
**Bookends** (The official supplier to the British Origami Society).
1-5 Exhibition Road
London
SW7 2HE
0207 589 2285

**Falkiner Fine Papers**
76 Southampton Row
London
WC1B 4AR
020 7831 1151

**Khadi Papers**
Unit 3
Chilgrove Farm
Chichester
West Sussex
PO18 9HU

**Paperchase**
213 Tottenham Court Road
London
W1P 9AF
020 7580 8496

**John Purcell Paper**
15 Rumsey Road
London
SW9 OTR
020 7737 5199

USA
**Colophon Book Arts Supply**
3611 Ryan Road, S.E.
Lacey, WA 98503
www.the gridnet/colophon

**Fascinating Folds**
P.O. Box 10070
Glendale
AZ 85318
800 968 2118

**Jerry's Artarama**
P.O. Box 58638J
Raleigh, NC 27658
800 968 2418
www.jerryscatalogue.com

**Nasco Arts and Crafts**
4825 Stoddard Road
Modesto, CA 95397
800 558 9595
www.nascofa.com

**Twinrocker Handmade Paper**
100 East 3rd Street
Brookston, IN 47923
800 757 8946
www.twinrock.com

AUSTRALIA
**A to Z Art Supplies**
50 Brunswick Terrace
Wynn Vale, SA 5127
08 8289 1202

**Art & Craft Warehouse**

19 Main Street

Pialba, QLD 4655

07 4124 2581

**Artland**

272 Moggill Road

Indooroopilly, QLD 4068

07 3878 5536

**Bondi Road Art Supplies**

181 Bondi Road

Bondi, NSW 2026

02 9386 1779

**Eckersleys**

126 Commercial Road

Prahran, VIC 3181

03 9510 1418

**Oxford Art Supplies Pty Ltd**

223 Oxford Street

Darlinghurst, NSW 2010

02 9360 4066

For further paper suppliers please contact the relevant national origami society, each of which has a supplies operation.

# Origami societies

**The British Origami Society:**
Started in 1967 by a small group of enthusiasts, and now boasting several hundred members worldwide, the BOS is devoted to the enjoyment and development of paperfolding. The society publishes a 40-page magazine every two months, holds regular meetings around England, and organizes two weekend conventions every year.

If you wish to contact the BOS, do so by writing to the membership secretary:

Mrs Penny Groom

2a The Chestnuts

Countesthorpe

Leicester LE8 5TL

UK

e-mail:

penny.groom@btinternet.com

www. britishorigami.org.uk

**Dansk Origami Centre** *(Denmark)*

c/o Thoki Yenn

Tranehavegard 1, St, tV

101-2450 Kobenhavn SV

Denmark

**M.F.P.P.** *(France)*

56 Rue Coriolis

75012 Paris

France

**Origami Deutschland EV** *(Germany)*

Postfach 1630

85316 Freising

Germany

**Origami Munchen** *(Germany)*

Postfach 22132

80503 Munchen 22

Germany

**Hungarigami** *(Hungary)*

Kecskemet pf 60

H6001

Hungary

**C.D.O.** *(Italy)*

P.O. Box 42,

21040 Caronno

Varesina

Italy

**Japan Origami Academic Society,**

c/o Gallery Origami House,

Asahi Mansion 2F

1-33-8-216 Hakusan

Bunkyo-ku

Tokyo 112

Japan

**Nippon Origami Association** *(Japan)*

2-064 Domir Gobancho,

12-gobancho

Chiyoda-ku

Tokyo 102-0076

Japan

**Origami Societeit Nederland**
*(The Netherlands)*

Maud Lambriex-Rousseau

Zilverlinde 38

NL-5237 HG's Hertogenbosch

The Netherlands

**Origami Munchen** *(Germany)*

Postfach 22132

80503 Munchen 22

Germany

**St. Petersburg Origami Centre**
*(Russia)*

Box 377

193318 St. Petersburg

Russia

**Association Espanola de Papiroflexia**
*(Spain)*

Apartado de Correos 13156

28080 Madrid

Spain

**Origami Sverige**
*(Sweden)*

c/o Dino Andreozzi

Tre Kallors Vag

145 65 Norsborg

Sweden

**Origami Switzerland**

Rue de Village 50

1214 Vernier

Switzerland

**Origami USA**

15 West 77th Street

New York

NY 10024 - 5192

CONTACTING THE AUTHOR:
If you wish to contact the author for details of workshops, commissions, or corporate bookings you can do so by post: 21 Woods Meadow, Thulston, Elvaston, South Derbyshire DE72 3UX.
telephone: 01332 574244   fax: 01332 758881   mobile: 07947 383029 or e-mail: Ricknbeech@AOL.com

# index

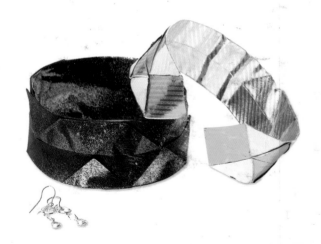